THE
HEAD
CASE

A young lawyer's journey to hold NFL Football
accountable for causing brain damage.

JASON LUCKASEVIC

ISBN 978-1-0980-4361-2 (paperback)
ISBN 978-1-0980-4362-9 (digital)

Christian Faith Publishing, Inc.
832 Park Avenue
Meadville, PA 16335
www.christianfaithpublishing.com

Printed in the United States of America

"When I discovered and reported the first cases of CTE in the brains of football players, other contact-sport athletes and military veterans, I was rejected, ridiculed, dehumanized, and ostracized. My depression got worse. I sank into a deep, dark and cold abyss. Jason Luckasevic stepped into my life and became a warm light in my lonely abyss. He picked me up, opened his door and invited me into the warmth of his heart, home, and family. He saved me. Without Jason, I do not think the world would have heard about CTE. He fought so hard to get the word out and enhance the humanity of every college football player and every NFL football player. He sacrificed all he had including his career to enhance this common humanity we all share. While every law firm or attorney he went to, in those early CTE days, sent him away, he kept the faith, fought silently and relentlessly to file the first massive lawsuit against the NFL on behalf of retired football players. I see Jason as a soldier of truth and integrity. With few more people like Jason, the world would no doubt become a more beautiful and perfect world. Thank you, Jason."

—Dr. Bennet Omalu,
Distinguished Service Award from the American Medical Association (AMA) for his work discovering CTE in American football players.

"Jason has gone above and beyond what anyone was willing to do, seek justice for men that gave their lives for the NFL. He has given my children hope that their father's death was not in vain and has helped many families seek the justice they deserve."

—Keana McMahon,
Former spouse of Justin Strzelczyk

"And we know that all things work together for good to those who love God, to those who are the called according to His purpose (Romans 8:28)."

—Vernon Maxwell,
Seven-year NFL veteran Linebacker and 1983
NFL Defensive Rookie of the Year

"As a lawyer, I can appreciate the struggles Jason encountered in even getting a case against the most successful and powerful sport's league in the world off the ground. Without Jason's courage to keep pushing and fighting against the NFL, former players and individuals across the world would not know about the dangers of repetitive head trauma and the long-term risk it causes to our population. Jason's story is a testament to his will, determination, and skill as a lawyer. Hopefully, this story empowers the next generation of lawyers and individuals across the globe to continue to stand up for what is right and continue the fight in the face of overwhelming and, at times, insurmountable adversity."

—Attorney Bob Cohen,
A Beverly Hills, California, family lawyer
Formerly a sports agent, who has represented football players including Vernon Maxwell

"We thank you for taking the greatest personal and a professional risk to represent our father, husband, and a friend (Mike Webster-HOF 1997) who died with CTE so that other players who suffered for years searching for an answer about their affections now had a name to their problem. Thank you for rewriting the last chapter to our glory in trouble life. The legacy Mike Webster's leave behind now will no longer tell the sad and horrific tale of a life torn apart before he died. Mike Webster will always and forever be a remembered as tremendous football player who, along with other former players, Mike left his greatest legacy off the field that other players and family can benefit from studying his brain. Thank you, Jason, for helping us."

—The Estate of Mike Webster, including his wife, children, and Sonny Jani

INTRODUCTION

Moses

"So you're going to be our Moses."

"Your what?" I exclaimed with a surprised and inquisitive tone in my voice. It's not everyday that a former NFL defensive rookie of the year, or anyone for that matter, approaches you with such a direct question.

"You're going to be our Moses" he repeated from his eye-popping six foot plus frame.

"Look, I don't know what you're talking about" I replied to this fifty years old giant of a man, whose bulging muscles and enormous frame looked like he could run circles around today's rookies at the NFL draft combine, as I wondered who or where he got the idea that I would embody one of the most famous biblical characters.

"I called Dr. Omalu after you gave me his phone number, and he told me 'let Jason be your Moses.'"

This conversation would lead to the eventual filing of a lawsuit that neither I, nor anyone in the legal profession or the world, could ever have imagined the vast ramifications. This former NFL player would go on to be my first client and the first named retired player to appear on the historic and earth-shattering lawsuit against the National Football League for its longstanding and systemic wrongful concealment of chronic brain injury former players suffered due to repetitive head trauma.

The lawsuit will forever be known as the "NFL Concussion Lawsuit" and it is, without a doubt, the most publicized and controversial lawsuit in the history of our country's jurisprudence in recent memory. More than the tobacco litigation, asbestos litigation,

7

and even major pharmaceutical drug cases, the "NFL Concussion Lawsuit" is the most misunderstood and culturally divisive litigation that I never thought I would ever be involved and the litigation that would forever change my personal and professional life.

The irony in what I remember as my "Moses conversation" with this former NFL player is that he too was a "Moses" for all former NFL players.

Vernon Maxwell is one of the leaders of former African American NFL players from the 1980s. Vernon battled all of the challenges life has thrown at him, from growing up near the hard-nosed Compton, California to excelling as an early round NFL Draft pick and eventual NFL Defensive Rookie of the Year. Without the courage that Vernon had to trust me with a lawsuit against the NFL for their decades long actions of concealing critical information about repetitive trauma and brain injury to players, without the courage he showed in standing up to the NFL, and without him asking me to be their Moses, all former NFL players and the world may not understand and appreciate concussions and repetitive brain injuries the way they do now.

Immediately after my conversation on this day with Vernon Maxwell, I called my personal and professional friend, Dr. Bennett Omalu, to ask him about calling me Moses. It is important to remember that at this point, Dr. Omalu, the Nigerian forensic pathologist who first found chronic traumatic encephalopathy (CTE) in former NFL players and threw the flag on the NFL, was on his way to having himself and his work immortalized in the Sony major motion picture *"Concussion"* where his life and story were portrayed by Will Smith. What Dr. Omalu said to me during this conversation has stayed with me as a badge of honor throughout my life.

"Jason, God fights my battles. Don't worry, the truth will set you free" he exclaimed. "You will be famous, and I will be able to say that I knew you when I was a nobody" he giggled through what I can only imagine was Dr. Omalu's big smile on the other end of the phone.

"Bennett...you're crazy. This is all because of you" I replied as I had many times before when talking to my friend. What I realized in that moment, and what I still remember to this day, is that what I was about to do from this one conversation with Vernon Maxwell, this one line where he asked me to be the Moses for all former NFL players, was the epitome of David vs. Goliath in our U.S. court system.

This book is an inside look into my journey through the NFL Concussion litigation and how it has influenced my personal and professional practice. Through this book you will learn about the ins and outs of high stakes litigation against the most successful and powerful organization in the world, the National Football League. You will learn about all of the triumphs and tragedies that have befallen former NFL players and one young lawyer who decided to take on the biggest industry in the world and won. Most of all, it is my hope that reading my story, it will inspire you to never back down and one day be a Moses for someone or something that needs justice.

CHAPTER 1

Growing Up

My name is Jason Luckasevic. I am a lawyer who practices in Pittsburgh, Pennsylvania. There are over one-and-a-quarter million lawyers in this country. I am the most unlikely person, let alone lawyer, you could have predicted that would have someday originated the NFL concussion litigation.

Before you start reading my book, I want to stress that I am not on a crusade to end the game of football. Rather, my obligation and responsibility as a lawyer remains the same as with any personal injury case that I handle which is to protect the injured from harm caused by another.

I grew up in Charleroi, Pennsylvania. Actually, to be specific, I lived in Fallowfield Township, a very rural community in the mid Monongahela Valley. As of the 2000 United States census, there were 4,600 residents with a median income of $45,000 per family from my small town. My little town in the mid-Mon Valley was known for its steel making and coke plants and exceptional football talent. After all, we lay claim to one of the NFL legends, Joe Montana.

Life was simple growing up in this small country town, formerly a farming community. Most locals weren't expected to leave town let alone ever make it big. You were expected to raise your family and continue to learn a trade and work in one of the local businesses.

My father, Ed, was a machinist in the local glass factory, Corning Glass. He always has been heavyset and had a full head of grey hair from as far back as I could recall. His parents were born and raised in

Charleroi of Baltic region of Poland and Slovakia decent. His dad was a World War II sergeant who saw combat in Germany. He later got involved in local politics and sold fruit and Christmas trees. My dad's mother lived until she was ninety-five years old, dying peacefully from Alzheimer's disease. She spent many years working in retail. My dad is the oldest of three siblings and is in his early seventies.

My father attended some college and achieved a two-year associate's degree from Robert Morris University in Pittsburgh. I best remember my dad working from seven in the morning until around three-thirty in the afternoon at the Charleroi glass factory and coming home with his dirty uniform. During most weekdays, he would pick up extra work as either a union official, or he spent time as a Fallowfield township supervisor, which was an elected position. He never seemed to have much time for our activities or even playing around the house. He was a busy man that worked hard to provide for our blue-collar family.

My mother, JoAnn, worked at a local credit union that handled the financial affairs of the local electric utilities which provided electric energy to the entire Monongahela Valley. She went back to work when I started the first grade. She attended some college courses with my father at Robert Morris University. She was very outgoing. Her job brought her in contact with many people who lived in the Mon Valley region. She recognized everyone from the community. If she wasn't caring for us, she spent time with her mother, who raised her alone and was also from the area. Her mother was eighty-nine years old when she recently passed from a short illness after never having been sick her entire life. From Slovakia decent, she worked until we made her retire in her seventies as a shipper at the glass factory plant in Charleroi.

My parents had two boys. My brother, Todd, is two years older than I am. From an early age, he was always more interested in hunting and fishing as opposed to sports. When I would play ball with the neighborhood kids, he would be out fishing in the pond about a half of a mile behind our house which abutted a cow pasture. We shared a bedroom with two twin beds in a small two-bedroom, two-bathroom home with a one-car garage and no air conditioning. But despite our different hobbies, my brother and I have remained very close to this very day.

My parents raised us very strictly. Despite their inability to do so, they believed that you could make it out of Charleroi onto bigger and better things. We had a curfew and rules to follow. You dared not break either.

I recall one time when my brother, myself, and one of our friends were out in the middle of the Monongahela River after midnight on a fishing boat without lights and with friends. I could have sworn that I would never see sunlight after that moment. And yes, hitting children was second nature. We got smacked around pretty good with a wooden paddle for not using our common sense and following their rules.

In truth, my parents knew what they were doing. In fact, my mom would tell everyone that she was going to raise a doctor and a lawyer.

The path to where I am today began earlier than normal for me. My neighbor friend, Josh, who lived on our dead-end street with less than twenty families, was about eight months older than I am. So he was ready to start kindergarten at Fallowfield Elementary school. My birthday fell at the very end of June. My parent's logic was to start me in school with Josh, otherwise I would have nothing to do all day long without my brother or any of the other kids who lived on the street who were already in school.

I would estimate, from what I have read, that the number of parents who redshirt their children is probably one in two today. That is the concept of starting your kids later at school so they are more developed physically and mentally. Instead, I was one of the youngest in my class. I used it as a major advantage and an opportunity to compete with older kids. It was my early motivation to keep up with the older kids and learn how to be competitive.

I was an above-average student. My grades were usually A's and B's. My intelligence was higher, which showed that I often underachieved with my class work. I tested into the gifted program. The program included about five kids from my class whose IQs tested above 125. The perk of being in this program allowed us to play games on the only two computers that the entire elementary school housed. Unfortunately, I was never trained well on how to use computers properly. However, I did excel at *Oregon Trail*.

I was never the top student in the class with the highest grades. There were around sixty kids in my grade at Fallowfield Elementary split into two sections. School came relatively easy for me. There never was a lot of studying.

I excelled at certain subjects like math and spelling. In fact, I always seemed to make it to the spelling bee finals in our elementary school. Ironically, one time I recall being eliminated near the final students for not spelling fraud correctly. I had included an *o* instead of an *a*. I'm sure that the NFL to this day wishes that word would not have stuck in my memory the rest of my life.

My excelling in math had a lot to do with my passion of sports. I was a sports junkie growing up. I would memorize every number and player of the Pittsburgh teams. I knew all their stats. I would either listen on the radio to the games or watch them on television. Then I would keep the box scores during the games.

Sports were big in our family and in my school. My grandfather, from an early age, would ask me to help him pick his weekly football bets using the point spreads. I guess I was pretty good at it as he always wanted to see me prior to Saturday and Sunday games with his sheet of paper in hand.

The holidays, especially Thanksgiving and Christmas, always surrounded football. I recall one of my favorite photos from about the age of ten was the first football jersey that I ever received. It was of a Dallas Cowboy at the time who wore #33. He was a University of Pittsburgh great and a local product. Years later, Tony Dorsett would become the most famous living spokesperson of this case against the NFL and my client and friend.

Sundays for the Luckasevic family were always left to church and football. We attended Mary, Mother of the Church in Charleroi, Pennsylvania. It was the local Catholic church. Then my brother and I would go off to CCD, otherwise known as Sunday school classes. Afterwards, the rest of the fall and winter days would be spent visiting relatives, watching football, and eating mom's home-cooked food. Sometimes in the evening, that included some local pizza to go with the evening games.

When you are from Pittsburgh, there was only the Steelers and church. If it snowed heavy, you would watch the Steelers; church could wait until next week. I loved watching the games. I would dream of someday being involved with sports. I realized I would never be good enough athletically. I still thought there would be an opportunity for me in sports whether through managing or broadcasting.

After school was out, I often spent time playing with the neighborhood kids in our yards. When we played football, we would each take a player's name. Everyone wanted to be a Steeler. The Steelers of the 1980s were aging from their championship years and were in a rebuilding phase. Their teams were average at best most years in the 1980s. I, however, secretly loved the New York Giants and their defense. They owned the greatest linebacker of all time, Lawrence "LT" Taylor. Years later, I never thought I would become close friends with one of the all-pro Giants from that historic defense, Leonard Marshall.

My school friends and I spent a lot of time playing deck hockey. We established a pretty good team that competed with the best around. Hockey was big in the early 1990s, with Mario Lemieux and the Pittsburgh Penguins franchise winning two Stanley Cup championships in the early 1990s. If we weren't playing hockey, we were off playing video games, some other sport or working.

Unfortunately, I had to work at an early age. My parents believed that exposing my brother and me to labor would instill in us a work ethic for excelling in school so we could use our brains toward a better job than having to spend our lives in the labor force. I did a lot of Christmas tree cutting and bailing trees on my grandfather's farm in Brownsville that sat on 150 acres. I spent a lot of time washing and waxing vehicles for family in the hot summers. I moved onto cutting grass for a few bucks in my early teens. My brother and I had a number of large country yards that we used the push mower to cut every week. At the legal age of sixteen, I took a job bussing tables and washing dishes at a local Elks lodge that held many a local banquet and celebration.

Ultimately, I graduated high school in 1994. I was an honor's student and finished approximately number 20 out of 125 students after we combined the students from the entire Charleroi area. Like grade school, high school to me was simple. I took the most advanced college preparation courses, but I never spent a lot of time on homework. Evenings were for sports or being outside or spending time with my friends.

I learned how to golf as a freshman in high school. I got pretty skilled at it without ever taking a single lesson. I made the all-section team as a junior and senior and even qualified for elite junior tournaments in the area. This led me to receive some interest and offers to play at some small NCAA Division 2 and Division 3 schools. I passed on those college choices so I could join my brother, who was at Washington and Jefferson College studying chemistry to become a doctor. I was going to enter their pre-law program to become, guess what, a lawyer.

My choice of college did not get me away from my small town. As John Mellancamp famously sang, "I was born in a small town, and I live in a small town, educated in a small town." At this point in my life, I figured that the world did not exist outside of my small Pittsburgh community.

CHAPTER 2

Meeting Dr. Bennet Omalu

The commissioner of the National Football League, Roger Goodell, is probably the most notable alumni from Washington and Jefferson College, a small NCAA Division III liberal arts college known for crafting students to become future doctors and lawyers.

The campus is spread over a small area of Washington, Pennsylvania, just about forty-five minutes south of Pittsburgh and less than twenty-five minutes from my family's house in Charleroi. I enrolled in the incoming class of 1998 with around 400 students. It was at this school where I received the best education imaginable and the greatest times of my life.

W&J College was known for getting their students into medical and law school with an almost perfect acceptance rate. However, to get those rates, their academic criteria is incredibly challenging such that they weed out students by the dozens. By the time you graduate, there were only about 250 students receiving diplomas during the commencement exercises.

To highlight this approach, I'll take you back to my brother's freshman year. He started in a small dormitory building that housed approximately twenty freshmen men on his floor. By the time he graduated, there was only one other person from that floor who graduated in the class of 1996. Most of his floor did not make it to their sophomore year at Washington and Jefferson College.

I went into college with the understanding that everyone who goes to law school majors in political science during their undergraduate schooling. However, after my first semester of college, I fell in love with English and ended up double majoring in English and political science. My personal favorite was always English literature with an emphasis in Shakespeare's works.

It was what happened after my first year that transformed the future and instilled in me the relentless approach of never giving up and never waiting to fail. After my freshman year, I was offered a summer job with a local politician. However, shortly before summer, the funding for the job fell through. Apparently, that is very typical for budgets involving state governments.

Not wanting to go back to a summer of washing cars and cutting grass, I was determined to do two things: lose the twenty pounds I gained my freshman year and take classes so that I could graduate early. I was racing every night to run with my high school classmate and friend who was a walk-on linebacker at the University of Pittsburgh. The other part was easier. I just needed to schedule as many college courses in the summer that I could manage.

I then decided to approach the academic dean at Washington and Jefferson College with my thought that I would like to graduate one year early with the class of 1997. I was told by the dean that no one graduates early at this college. Everyone thinks they can, but it is a very challenging endeavor.

When I returned my sophomore year, I had shed those twenty pounds. I always carried extra weight, which ran in my family. I returned as a sophomore, plus the extra summer classes, at my consistent weight of 190 pounds at 6 feet tall. When I returned to college, I started a job title searching for a Charleroi law firm of Bassi & Associates at the Washington Courthouse while I was taking more than the required credits during the school year.

My brother and our friends all graduated that year with the class of 1996. They all went on to medical school and became doctors in various specialties. In the meantime, I came back for my junior-senior year still working at the Bassi law firm and holding down more than the required credits.

It's at that time that my life would change forever. During that first week back to school, one of my friends introduced me to some of the incoming freshmen women who moved to the top floor of our dormitory. One in particular caught my eye. She was petite, but her smile was very warm and welcoming. Her confidence and intelligence and overall friendly attitude struck me. To make a long story short, she, at the time named Kelly Gablick, has been my inspiration to become smarter every day.

By example, every incoming freshman must take a political science course taught by the department chair, Dr. Joseph DiSarro. He notoriously gives out one A per semester. I struggled to get a B or C in his class—that was how difficult it was to me. I knew that I had to marry Kelly when I learned that she got an A in his class.

I was able to prove the dean wrong, and I graduated from Washington and Jefferson College class of 1997 one year early from my initial class. Once again, I was the example that redshirting kids was overrated. Rather, I was now two years younger than my classmates who were entering Duquesne Law School class of 2000. Over the summer, I turned legally old enough to drink alcohol, and I was working at Bassi's law firm. Most importantly, I was spending all of my free time with Kelly.

As much as college was the best years of my life, law school was the worst years. I really didn't know what I had gotten myself into. The professors seemed miserable. The material and teaching style of never giving you the answers to the questions didn't make any sense. Most students were cold and overly competitive. They seemed to have their job choices and type of law they wanted to practice already decided. This may have been from the fact that so many of my classmates were second-generation lawyers-to-be.

My classmates would sit in the library or the common areas in the one building that housed the law school in downtown Pittsburgh all day long trying to show you how much they understood about a United States Supreme Court case that was decided many decades ago. Then, they would scramble to put together outlines for each class and would volunteer to answer every question during the classes.

This type of mentality just wasn't for me. I needed to find out if I made the right decision. I therefore sought to get a job in the legal profession and explore my passion of sports and entertainment law. I figured that I would be the next Jerry McGuire. I figured that it could not be that difficult to get into the field of sports law in Pittsburgh.

I was fortunate enough to find a legal job as a law clerk by the very end of my first year of law school. I started in May 1998 at Goldberg, Persky & White. It was a firm that helped injured asbestos victims, just like the commercials you see on television advertising for mesothelioma victims. Going into the job, I had very little information about asbestos. In fact, I didn't understand much about civil litigation at all. It's probably because I didn't grow up with a family or friends who were lawyers. This job was my first experience as to how important and critical networking is in the professional arena.

I was led to Goldberg, Persky & White from our very close family friend, Jerry Strelick. Jerry grew up long-time friends with my dad and his side of the family. Jerry was critical in me obtaining this job as he was the president of the U.S. Steel Clairton Works union and dealt with some of Goldberg, Persky & White's senior partners. He helped me secure an interview, and from there, I ran with the job opportunity that I was given.

In the meantime, in law school, I got involved with the sports and entertainment law society. We put on lectures and did various activities where we met the who's who of local lawyers involved with representing players, teams, and musicians as well. I learned quickly that this would be a difficult field to crack as there were only two Pittsburgh sports agents and a few other established lawyers helping with the local sports franchises.

I therefore decided that working hard at Goldberg, Persky & White was my ticket to the legal profession. It seemed like a place that was a perfect fit for me. The staff was happy, friendly, and always joking with each other. The firm held regular parties, and the lawyers all talked to each other and drove nice cars. My ambition was to work thirty to thirty-five hours during the school week and fifty-plus hours during the summer. So that is exactly what I did. I was assigned to help research, write, and draft various pleadings for their cases.

My strategy of putting work before law school worked out for me. My grades were not competitive with the other law students to say the least. I graduated number 100 out of 103 students. I, however, was offered a job at Goldberg, Persky & White.

I was transferred into the Western Pennsylvania asbestos department and assigned to Janice Savinis to be my boss at Goldberg, Persky & White. At that time in the fall of 2000, Janice was a single female in her early forties who lived with her parents. She carried a loud voice. She was hard working, and she was tough.

I received notice that I passed the bar examination on a Friday in October. The very next week, I was sworn in to practice law, with Janice sponsoring me during a swearing in procedure with the clerk of the prothontary's office. On Friday of that week, I drove to Johnstown to start depositions of former employees who were clients of my firm involving their diagnosis of asbestosis and their exposure to asbestos materials at the Bethlehem Steel facility in Johnstown. For the next six months, I was tasked with driving my Honda Civic to Johnstown from my Brookline apartment for ninety minutes and covering two or three depositions per day. In the meantime, I was figuring out all about the largest steel producing plant in the United States that sprawled over nine miles of the Johnstown area while learning how to litigate an asbestos case. This required me to constantly contact the other lawyers at the firm to ask questions after each deposition was completed.

In the meantime, my brother was in medical school doing internships covering various medical specialties all around the country. Some of them were not the most desirable locations. One time, he was in a rough city delivering babies for a young white couple. As typically happens in the movies, the baby came out darker than both parents.

Eventually, Todd's tour of specialties took him to the Allegheny County Medical Examiner's office, where he was supposed to learn from the famous Dr. Cyril Wecht. Dr. Wecht is most known for his findings as to the cause of death of John F. Kennedy, Jon Bennet Ramsey, and Anna Nicole Smith, to name a few. However, the reality was that Dr. Wecht was so busy in his personal pursuits that he was rarely present at the county medical examiner's office.

As a result, my brother was trained by Dr. Bennet Omalu, who was working as one of the assistant medical examiners. Dr. Omalu was of Nigerian decent who came to the states to explore his interest in pathology. He was a warm-spirited young man who loved the educational aspects of determining the cause of someone's death. He thought of himself as a voice for the dead. He also loved educating himself. He held board certifications in forensic, anatomic, clinical, and neuropathology. These are specialties of doing autopsies, making diagnosis of the dead, as well as brain and spinal cord deaths. Dr. Bennet Omalu was schooled in epidemiology, the study of the causes of diseases. He even went on to obtain a master's degree in business administration from Carnegie Mellon University.

Dr. Omalu and Todd hit it off instantly. Dr. Omalu loved Todd's passion and interest in doing autopsies. Dr. Omalu believed that my brother was a natural for this area of medical specialty as he caught on quickly and was organized. Maybe it was because of my brother's filleting game he hunted and caught for many years. Todd also found someone he could spend some time with after hours in the city. They both seemed to be loners who did not have many friends or acquaintances in the area after Bennet being new and Todd bouncing around the country for many years. The two of them would go out for food, drinks, and even an occasional hockey game.

Sports always came before school for me. During the 1990s and into the 2000s, the Pittsburgh Penguins offered a student rush program for any college student and offered the best available seats for $20. On one occasion, my brother asked if I would like to join Bennet and him at a Penguin's game during a week night. I never passed on these opportunities. As they say, the rest is history.

Dr. Omalu and I saw each other's passions instantly. I knew that he was motivated to be the best in his profession. Likewise, I think he saw someone in me who has a knack for speaking and was passionate about helping others and growing in the legal profession.

Over the years, our paths would continue to cross through my brother. One time, he came over during the holidays to our home in

Charleroi. There were other times we would grab a drink downtown. Sometimes I would call and ask him medical questions that related to matters that were ongoing in my cases. I felt that it was very important to keep him as a contact and acquaintance as I never knew where networking with him could lead.

Eventually, serendipity led Dr. Omalu to one day have the body of "Iron" Mike Webster arrive at his medical examiner's office on a weekend. Mike Webster was the heart of the Pittsburgh Steelers during the 1970s. He played over fifteen seasons in the NFL as the all-pro starting center who crouched at the center of their four Super Bowl titles in the 1970s. After football, he was equally known for his reclusive and strange life as he was for being elected into the NFL Hall of Fame.

Bennet knew to examine Mike's brain for chronic injury. Upon performing his autopsy, Dr. Omalu was shocked to find that Mike Webster's brain appeared normal to his naked eye. After many tests and months of studying his findings, Bennet diagnosed Mike Webster as dying from chronic traumatic encephalopathy, which he named as CTE. It was a disease of dementia specifically caused from years of head trauma from playing professional football.

I was very aware of Bennet's diagnosis of Mike Webster with CTE. I knew this because it gained a tiny amount of exposure in the local media at the time. I didn't give it much thought at the time. My only thoughts were that I suspected that Bennet would move onto a successful career as a pathologist following in the steps of his famous mentor, Dr. Cyril Wecht. Regarding his diagnosis, I also didn't think much of it. It wasn't surprising. Playing football was much akin to being a boxer. Everyone knows that Muhammad Ali suffered from debilitating brain damage. After all, my mom never wanted us to play football for fear of hurting ourselves. I never thought this conclusion by Dr. Omalu would ever be called into question.

My brother eventually finished his training and moved onto be an assistant medical examiner in Richmond, Virginia, and, later, Alexandria, Virginia.

In the meantime, I was helping Jack Tierney, a lawyer winding down his career at my law firm, with some employment discrimination and ERISA pension cases. I also was moving up the ladder on my asbestos case load as well as working long and difficult hours as the youngest associate under Janice Savinis. Occasionally, I would run into some personal injury cases that I brought into the firm and would successfully handle them to a fair resolution. My networking abilities led me to those opportunities outside of the asbestos practice.

CHAPTER 3

My Family

In the summer of 2002, I married Kelly Gablick. She had just completed her second year of law school at Duquesne University. We were living in separate apartments in Brookline, which is two miles from downtown Pittsburgh, across the street from each other during this period of time after she graduated from Washington and Jefferson College. Brookline was a city of Pittsburgh community that was a very old neighborhood with many qualities that made it safe. The top reason of which was that many of the city police force lived in Brookline.

Our wedding was a beautiful and relatively small ceremony that took place at the Duquesne University church and was conducted by our priest from St. Pius X church in Brookline.

The reception was attended by about 140 close friends and family at a hotel in downtown Pittsburgh. My brother, of course, was my best man.

We took a Disney vacation afterwards to Disneyworld and a Disney cruise. I doubt I will ever get Kelly back on a cruise ship after that trip as she disliked the rocking of the ship. When we came back home, it was truly an amazing moment to realize that the Luckasevic family would soon have two lawyers in our blue-collar family.

Also, during this period of time, my parents remained very close and supportive of my brother and myself. It didn't seem like a week went by without my parents insisting on visiting me in Pittsburgh or my brother near Washington DC. It always seemed as though they had an excuse to drive forty-five minutes to downtown Pittsburgh regularly.

My job as a young associate at Goldberg, Persky & White remained incredibly busy. I was climbing the ladder with each case I handled successfully.

I was being trained by some excellent trial lawyers in Janice Savinis and Aaron DeLuca and I still had Jack Tierney throwing me some meaningful work on his endeavors. By 2003, I was regularly assisting Janice and Aaron in trials. I put important witnesses on the stand during trials and took all the critical depositions to develop the exposures in the case as it related to the specific companies that were on trial. Aaron and I particularly made a great team. Maybe it was the fact that he graduated from Charleroi about six years prior to me.

Aaron DeLuca was on the fast track to success. I figured tying my career path to him was a good strategical game plan. We had just finished working up one of the largest settlements in Allegheny County on an asbestos case. He was in the process of being promoted to partner. I was glad because he deserved it, and he would actually speak highly of my efforts to his new partners.

Just when everything was starting to go smoothly, everything suddenly and unexpectedly changed. Aaron was offered a job in Houston, Texas, with Mark Lanier in late 2003. He left our law firm and asked if I wanted to join him. I had to pass on this opportunity to work for Mark Lanier, who was one of the most successful trial lawyers in the country. My decision was again based on the fact that I could not leave my hometown.

Two months later, I helped Janice Savinis try a case to a $6-million verdict in Allegheny County. I think in large part the award was based on my creative idea to have the exposure expert testify to how many million fibers the plaintiff breathed. The law in the Commonwealth of Pennsylvania prohibits someone from asking the jury to award a certain dollar amount during closing arguments. I along with our material science expert created an example of how many asbestos fibers the victim breathed in one day by doing an elaborate calculation in front of the jury. This number was again reiterated by Janice in the closing argument. The jury came back in a few hours with half of the dollar value of the exposure amount we showed them and Janice reminded them of during the closing argument.

Immediately after that verdict, Janice and two other lawyers left Goldberg, Persky & White to open their own practice down the street. She was tired of the politics of law and wanted to control her own destiny. She had asked me to join them. At this stage in my career, I couldn't take the professional risk. After all, I was happy at Goldberg, Persky & White. Nonetheless, in a matter of a couple of months, I was completely stunned to have lost my two closest mentors in Aaron and, now, Janice.

This adversarial process with two of my closest mentors was my first glimpse as a young lawyer into the competitive and contentious disputes amongst members of our profession. The lessons that I learned from this incident would inform my experiences in dealing with defense lawyers and members of the plaintiff's bar later in my career when I began to tackle the largest case against the largest corporation I could ever imagine.

A few months later, I received a call from Aaron DeLuca during this trying time period late one evening. It seemed as though I never made it home in the evenings or weekends as there was so much extra work during this transitional period of time. Aaron told me of another opportunity. He had a friend in New York that was looking for someone like me. I again passed on the opportunity as I believed that Pittsburgh was the only place I wanted to be. Pittsburgh was home. It was my small town.

I had just lost two mentors in a matter of months. I knew that I would have to become a lawyer who could stand on his own two feet real quick. I no longer had their leadership. I no longer had people to ask for help in my department. I needed to figure it out for myself. Once again, it reminded me of my experience as a young student entering school. I was now the young guy who had to stand on his own two feet with the older and more experienced gang.

By end of 2004, I was trying cases on my own. My brother was getting married to add a third lawyer to the family. And, my parents started thinking about moving out of Charleroi and being closer to us. My dad was starting a new job, and my mom was happy thinking about the fact that she only had a few more years before she could retire.

In the meantime, Kelly and I moved south of Brookline and Pittsburgh to the south hills community. We purchased a starter 2,500 square-foot house in South Fayette, which is about a twenty-five-minute drive from downtown Pittsburgh. I also finally joined a country club on a discounted under-forty membership rate. I was ready to get back to my passion of golfing and maybe be competitive at golf again someday.

CHAPTER 4

Trial in Indiana

A new boss, Peter Paladino, was appointed to oversee the Western Pennsylvania asbestos practice after Janice and Aaron had left. Many of the partners referred to him as "The Hammer." He was a nice, smart, Catholic attorney who started in the early days of Goldberg, Persky & White law firm.

I got to know Pete pretty quickly because he was thrown into a number of cases, and he had no choice but to be open to and rely on my suggestions and advice. We hit it off pretty well. I think it had a lot to do with the fact that we both came from solid blue-collar family backgrounds and we liked to golf.

Instantly, Pete felt at ease with my capabilities. I was working up cases for trial, I was getting equal results to Janice and Aaron on their past cases when they were with the firm, and I was leading the younger lawyers by example.

By 2005, Pete felt that he no longer needed to watch over me at trials. I was completely on my own.

At that time, I was working on a case in Indiana County, Pennsylvania. This is a rather small and very conservative rural county about two hours East of Pittsburgh. Their beautiful courthouse sits next to the Jimmy Stewart museum. Walking into the town and courthouse, it was like stepping into *It's a Wonderful Life*. Time certainly stood still there for many years.

I was working on a lawsuit involving a guy who died in his early seventies after working at a Fisher Scientific plant. They were a company that made the laboratory equipment, burners, hoods, and ovens found in many high school chemistry classes.

My client was tasked with using power saws to cut the insulation in the hoods and ovens to fit properly. This insulation was a cement board material that was full of the most toxic asbestos fiber type. It was placed inside the hoods and ovens to provide insulation to withstand very high temperatures.

Leading up to this trial, I had been asked on countless occasions by Dr. Omalu to work as an expert for me. Bennet would always call and say, "Jason, let me show you what I can do on these asbestos cases." I would put him off and tell him that I would look around for a case or two. I was concerned that jurors and lawyers would have bias toward him since he was from Nigeria. I was also concerned that he didn't have experience in these cases in that he would not properly understand the science and medicine surrounding asbestos diseases.

Ultimately, because of his persistence, I gave in to trying him out. I gave him a couple of cases that were not trial listed first. I figured he could not hurt those cases. If he did poorly, well, I could always go back to the same old recycled experts that every law firm in the country was using.

I was blown away with his written report. I figured that there was no way possible that this person who was difficult to understand due to his thick Nigerian accent would be able to write better than any expert physician I have ever read a report from. But he did.

The report was over fifteen pages in length. It was well written, analyzed, and supported with countless references and citations, all the things lawyers hope that their experts would do in a legal case. After that first attempt, I started to use him more frequently. Typically, I would search out cases that I knew would not try to a jury verdict. I especially liked the fact that he worked so quickly. He helped me meet my court deadlines ahead of schedule so as to avoid any added stress.

This case in Indiana was one of those cases that was not supposed to go to a jury verdict. However, the climate changed with one of the defendants. They were running out of insurance coverage, and they could not afford to pay the typical demand to settle such a serious death case.

Their attorney, Matt Wimer, was one of the best in the business. He had over thirty years of experience trying civil cases. He was in the Academy of Trial lawyers for our legal community. He spent parts of his legal practice time on my side of the fence representing medical malpractice victims. Matt Wimer was as nice and as honest an attorney that you could ever meet. A true nightmare of an opponent to try a case against. This combination added to my anxiety, and there was also the reality that my expert was Dr. Omalu.

After openings on the first day of trial, I had another attorney from my law firm, Jason Shipp, helping with some of the legal issues and putting on a couple witnesses. That evening, we went to dinner with Dr. Omalu and the same material science expert who helped us win a $6-million verdict a year prior. After dinner, I needed to spend time preparing Dr. Omalu for testimony. However, he wasn't paying any attention to me because Jason Shipp and the other expert were downstairs at the hotel bar having a few drinks.

Dr. Omalu kept saying, "Don't worry, this will be fine." He kept telling me that "I would do a good job." I was ready to strangle him. What had I gotten myself into? I was going to do a good job? What difference does that make if "I do a good job" and he doesn't know how to testify in an asbestos case? Finally, his persistence of ignoring me and insisting on having a drink won. I gave up and let him go drinking while I pondered how to ask him questions that required one-word answers.

After Jason Shipp and our star experts spent the evening drinking, I figured we were in for it when no one made it to breakfast on time. Off I drove, by myself, to the courthouse with hopes that Jason Shipp would bring our two star expert witnesses on time with at least a gallon of coffee inside them. Fortunately, they showed up with a minute to spare.

The trial judge looked at me and asked, "Are you ready to call your next witness, Mr. Luckasevic?" Judge Greg Olson was a polite and very professional judge that expected the lawyers to be prepared and timely.

I answered, "Plaintiff's call Dr. Bennet Omalu." Those words may have been the last thing I said for the next hour. Dr. Omalu was completely captivating. He showed the jurors, literally with diagrams, taking off his suit coat, acting and pointing how my client was exposed to asbestos, how the lungs worked, and how it killed him. I swear that he didn't even have an accent. He was so polite and friendly. It was as if he personally knew every single juror.

I don't even recall Matt Wimer asking him any questions on cross-examination. When Bennet was done, I pulled him aside during the lunch break and asked, "How did you learn to do that?"

He responded that "I did a very good job and I am a good lawyer." I once again just shook my head at him and bid him farewell and thanks.

Two days later, I was giving my closing argument. I recall it quite well, 'you will be asked by your friends and relatives if the case you served on was interesting? Did your verdict make a difference? That is the question you will have to answer, did your verdict make a difference? And, with that, I leave my client in your hands.'

While the jury was out for a few hours, I thought to myself, *Well, I'm twenty-eight years old, I have now tried cases all by myself, and now I found a new star witness for my law firm's cases.* Dr. Omalu was incredible. He was entirely believable and sincere. I was glad my brother introduced him to me. We could make a great team. Little did I know what was to come in the future.

The jury came back awarding my client one of the largest sums of money ever in this very conservative county. The thing that struck me the most is that I remember talking to Judge Olson about his conversation with the jurors. He said that the jurors felt like experts. They believed that they could diagnose lung problems and knew more about asbestos exposures and the workings of the human body than ever before. The jurors absolutely loved Dr. Omalu.

I called my brother that evening to tell him about Bennet. He just laughed and said, "I told you that he knows what he is doing. Bennet is the man." He told me that I had a good person and witness in Bennet and that I should keep using him. "He is a good person to know." Did that ever turn out to be the biggest understatement?

CHAPTER 5

Dr. Omalu's Discovery

By the end of 2006, Dr. Omalu diagnosed Mike Webster, Andre Waters, Terry Long, and Justin Strzelczyk with chronic traumatic encephalopathy. They were the original four former NFL players who themselves unknowingly died for scientific advancement.

It all started when Dr. Omalu examined Mike Webster when he was in the medical examiner's office in Pittsburgh because it was his on-call day to handle the weekend autopsies. Mike Webster is widely regarded as one of the greatest offensive linemen to play the game of football. He was the NFL Hall of Fame center for the Pittsburgh Steelers for 17 seasons and helped lead the Steeler's dynasty to four Super Bowl championships in the 1970s.

Mike Webster became the poster child of the brain-injured football players. After his career, he lived a well-documented juxtaposed life as described in the media. He often lived in his vehicle. He failed to remember many of his appointments or events. He typically ended up in strange locations such as different states, and he often was found sleeping in his truck in train stations. He required heavy amounts of medication to get him through a typical day. Sometimes, he or a friend would use a taser gun to shock him to sleep.

Dr. Omalu later described Mike Webster's brain as appearing normal upon visual examination. If you have never seen an autopsy, it is a shocking experience. They literally dissect the body of a human much like we dissect a frog in high school biology class. For humans, they take out every body part and examine it and then take samples to create slides to view tissue specimens microscopically.

In Webster's case, Dr. Omalu pealed the skin off of the face of Mike Webster and used a saw to cut his skull and remove his brain. He was surprised that it appeared normal to the human eye as brains of boxers historically have visual damage. Dr. Omalu therefore decided to create slides, and after they were prepared weeks later, they showed the changes he suspected. Mike Webster's brain had tangles or clumps of tau protein buildup which aged his brain much like a person in his eighties suffering from chronic Alzheimer's dementia. Mike Webster, however, was only fifty when he died. He has no heredity brain disease in his family. His only causative connection was repeated brain trauma from decades of football.

The Webster family was in the midst of a legal action against the NFL Bert Bell/Pete Rozelle disability plan at the time. Their lawyer, Bob Fitzsimmons, was a courageous bulldog of an attorney with extensive personal injury experience from Wheeling, West Virginia. Attorney Fitzsimmons was engulfed in a heated dispute with the disability system. The battle surrounded whether Mike Webster's injuries were compensable and were football-related. The second hurdle was that the NFL was arguing that the Mike Webster could not prove that his brain injury actually started many years earlier.

Ultimately, Bob Fitzsimmons and the Webster family will go down in history to first challenge the NFL on the issue of trauma causing football's dementia. After many years, the Websters and Attorney Fitzsimmons prevailed over the NFL disability system and were awarded over a million dollars.

Terry Long was a former NFL offensive guard for the Pittsburgh Steelers. While in college, he was a standout wrestler at East Carolina University. He played seven years in the NFL. Terry also had a few off-field issues.

He was suspended in 1991 for violating the NFL's steroid policy. At that time, he unsuccessfully attempted suicide. He struggled in his post-retirement life. His marriage to Lynne was always on the rocks, and his business decisions and affairs were misguided and erratic. Terry took his life in 2005 by drinking antifreeze. This was shortly after a federal grand jury indicted him on charges that he fraudulently obtained loans for a chicken-processing plant which he owned and allegedly burned to the ground to collect insurance money.

As irony would have it, Terry Long's forty-four-year-old body ended up on the Allegheny County medical examiner's office in the hands of Dr. Bennet Omalu. Terry Long's brain illustrated that he again he had chronic traumatic encephalopathy from years of playing football. His brain appeared twice as old as his age.

By early 2006, Chris Nowinski published a book entitled *Head Games: Football's Concussion Crisis*. Chris was a former WWE wrestler whose career was cut short due to post-concussion syndrome in 2003. Around that time, he came across Dr. Omalu and some other leading concussion experts and formed a non-profit called the Sports Legacy Institute. The mission was to study chronic traumatic encephalopathy.

In late 2006, Andre Waters was found dead from a gunshot wound to his head. Andre was best known as a ferocious hitter as a defensive back who played eleven seasons in the NFL, mainly with the Philadelphia Eagles. In fact, the league created a rule unofficially termed the "Andre Waters rule," prohibiting hits to quarterbacks below the waist when they are out of the pocket. He was on one of the notoriously best defenses during the early 1990s and was endeared with the nickname "Dirty Waters."

After football, Andre struggled with relationships. He disappeared from contact with friends and failed to ever obtain a coaching position in the NFL that he so desired. At the age of forty-four, his brain was sought by Chris Nowinski for testing by Dr. Bennet Omalu.

Dr. Omalu, this time, examined the remaining pieces of Andre's brain and determined that it had degenerated into that of an eighty-five-year-old man with similar characteristics to those of early-stage Alzheimer's victims and again described it as CTE. Andre was only forty-four years old.

The fourth victim was Justin Strzelczyk. Justin was an offensive lineman for the Pittsburgh Steelers playing nine seasons in the NFL. Despite being an eleventh-round draft pick, he played in 133 career games coming out of the University of Maine. He was very well liked because he was a team player that helped the Steelers reach the super bowl in 1995.

After his career, Justin bounced around from different interests, including dealing in businesses involving foods such as buffalo wings and barbeque sauces. Justin enjoyed riding Harley Davidson motorcycles. He played guitar and banjo. Like the others, he, as well, lost a lot of money in his business endeavors, including one that was a daycare business. Justin had citations for driving under the influence, and he was once arrested for carrying a firearm without a permit. Ultimately, he divorced his wife, Keena, in 2001 after they had two children.

Justin died in a fiery automobile crash when he drove the wrong way on a highway into a tank truck at a speed of ninety miles per hour in 2005. It was reported that he was hearing voices at the time, causing him bizarre behavior. Many believe Justin was speeding to avoid the voices that were chasing him. Justin's brain was recovered by Chris Nowinski and was given to Dr. Omalu to examine. Dr. Bennet Omalu found that Justin suffered CTE brain damage from his years of playing football.

Dr. Omalu was off to publish all four of those autopsy findings as medical and scientific breakthroughs. He, a young man from Nigeria, believed he had established a new chronic brain disease linked to professional football. This would make the world happy—or so he thought.

CHAPTER 6

Next Case—Meeting with Dr. Omalu

One thing that I learned in the practice of civil litigation is that doctors love to work as experts. I am not sure if it is because the healthcare system does not adequately compensate them enough to pay for all of their student loan debt or because they love to show everyone how much they know.

Dr. Omalu was no different. As a young professional, Bennet loved to work private medical legal cases on the side. It helped fill his free time and allowed him an opportunity to supplement his modest income as a county medical examiner.

After that trial in Indiana, I was the biggest fan of Bennet that you could imagine. I was ready to use him in any case of mine going forward. I was also marketing him to other lawyers throughout the country to use him as their expert.

It was convenient to have a friend that served as your expert. You could call him for simple questions and advice at no charge. He always picked up his cellphone when I called; he still does it to this day. I loved the fact that Bennet would show up at my office down the street from his place of work often unannounced.

Bennet had a habit of coming to my law firm's office about five city blocks away from the medical examiner's office to deliver his completed report. Then he would ask me to give him the next case to work on while he was there. This showed his good business sense which made it hard for me to say no. Not that I would even want to.

Around late 2006, I had the habit of coming to the office at 6:00 a.m. every day. I'm not sure where I picked up the habit. It could have been from Janice, who worked seven days a week and never missed a day of work. It could have been from my lack of patience in sitting in traffic. Or it could be because I refused to fail. I wanted to be successful. My mom always had a saying that she instilled in my brother and me; "the harder you work now, the easier the rest of your life will be." I believed that. Therefore, I made sure that every day as a lawyer, I was the first person in the office. To this day, I always strive to outwork everyone.

When I got to the office, I had my one cup of caffeine while reading the Pittsburgh Post-Gazette. It was around September 2006, and the morning's headlines read, "Steelers doctor says concluding football led to Long's demise is bad science." It was a long article that quoted the Pittsburgh Steeler team neurosurgeon, Dr. Joseph Maroon, as saying that Dr. Omalu's findings of CTE were just "bad science." Rather, Dr. Maroon believed that drug abuse and suicide attempts were causative of Terry Long's demise.

That wasn't all, the article then quoted Dr. Elliott Pellman, the chair of the NFL's mild traumatic brain injury committee. Dr. Pellman was quoted as saying that Dr. Omalu's conclusions were "speculative and unscientific."

This article struck me as a nuclear attack on Dr. Omalu. One of the classes I truly enjoyed in law school was trial advocacy. It was a class on courtroom trial skills taught by President Judge of the Common Pleas Court in Allegheny County, Judge Jeffrey Manning, while in my last year at Duquesne University Law School. It, by far, was one of my few favorite memories of the law school learning process. Judge Manning taught many criminal and civil trial lawyers who attended Duquesne Law School and later became world-class trial attorneys. He was once an outstanding criminal trial prosecuting lawyer and then moved on to handle every major death penalty case as the presiding trial judge in Allegheny County.

Judge Manning always gave a lecture at the end of the semester. His most important point that he drove across was that, when we become lawyers, we must practice with integrity. We must practice with honesty and have strong moral principles. This conversation stuck with me. The problem with lawyers has always been their dishonesty. Just look no further than the dishonesty jokes. We've all heard them. How does an attorney sleep? First, he lies on one side, and then he lies on the other. Shamefully, there are too many dishonest and immoral lawyers. We will talk about those types of lawyers later in this book.

The principal of integrity is no different for the medical profession. When you call someone unscientific, when you say that they practice bad science, you are saying they are immoral and dishonest. In essence, as a medical professional, they completely lack integrity.

I knew Bennet was an honest person. After all, the famous Dr. Cyril Wecht believed in Bennet's findings. I knew that all Bennet did was look at brain slices under a microscope. He had nothing to gain by lying. He only had everything to lose by making up or faking a medical condition related to a sport.

His conclusion, after all, was not preposterous. This condition had existed for decades in the brains of boxers. I could not understand why Doctors Maroon and Pellman made those remarks. Did they really believe that football didn't cause head injury? Did they believe that Dr. Omalu was a fraud? Did they know something about him that my brother or I had not uncovered? Or was this an effort to hide something on behalf of the football leagues?

When Bennet came to my office that morning during football season in 2006, this time, we had a meeting planned around 7:00 a.m. I immediately started our conversation with discussing the morning's newspaper article. I remember asking him if his ears were ringing. Then I asked him why the NFL's doctors were saying those negative things.

For the first time, he shared with me the hostilities that he had been receiving behind the scenes. I felt like I was the first person he opened up to about these issues. I was completely unaware that the NFL had sent out their people to immediately discredit Bennet's findings. They were attacking him in the media. They were attacking him in the medical and scientific community.

I told Bennet that he needed to do something about this. It was very clear to me that the NFL was trying to cover up something. I'll never forget what he said next. He looked at me very seriously and said, "Jason, you are a good lawyer. You figure this out."

I laughed and told him, "There are two problems. I don't have any time, and I don't have any clients." He asked me if I would look into it. I told him I would do him that favor as a friend if I could get in touch with some former players or their spouses.

He left my office after we talked for a short while about the asbestos case he just finished his expert narrative report on, and of course, I found him another case to handle, and my law firm paid his invoice for his time. I figured that was the last conversation that I would ever have with Bennet on the subject of the NFL and CTE. I was very wrong with that thought.

CHAPTER 7

NFL and Perception

There are many differences between the NFL and the tobacco companies. The biggest difference is that cigarettes taste like, well, cigarettes and the NFL tastes like mom's home-made apple pie. Football has become American's sport and pastime. It took over the ratings years ago from baseball. It hosts the largest television event in the world. It holds every top ten television spot in the United States' television markets ahead of every television show and sitcom.

Companies pay millions and billions of dollars to sponsor the league. The National Football League does not pay a penny for a single commercial or entertainment icon at the Super Bowl. Not only does the NFL not pay a penny to the entertainers who perform during the Super Bowl pre-game and halftime shows; in 2014, the league actually tried to coerce the entertainers to sign over a percentage of their post-Super Bowl earnings in the belief that the exposure of appearing on the NFL broadcast directly enhances the entertainer's earning power.

Fans pay countless sums of money to attend games, tailgate, and own merchandise of their teams. No one protects their brand more aggressively than the NFL. The mantra, "Protect the Shield," is more than a catchphrase; it is a business model that touches every single aspect of NFL operations. Federal agents from the FBI, U.S. Customs, and other federal agencies routinely conduct raids, seizing millions of dollars' worth of counterfeit NFL merchandise. Meanwhile, the NFL has become the mecca of the gambling world, with betting and fantasy football leagues covering every aspect of the league and individual players and now permitted in every state in the country.

Arguably the NFL grew to its great stature through marketing violence. It captured the imagination of fans by glorifying the athletes through their speed, power, and physicality. The NFL appears well on its way to having live football games on television seven nights a week during the season, which also appears to be increasing in length due to Commissioner Roger Goodell's stated desire to attain a goal of eighteen games per season. During recent seasons, live NFL games are televised on Sunday, Monday, Thursday, and Saturday.

Today, the NFL sits at the pinnacle of professional sports as a multi-billion-dollar empire. In 2010, Commissioner Roger Goodell set a goal for the NFL to triple its annual revenue within the next seventeen years. To achieve this goal, the NFL will require more games, expanded playoffs, more luxury seats, suites, and amenities that high-roller fans will have to absorb the price tag.

The NFL was crafted in the 1960s as a combination of the AFL and NFL. They unionized in 1969. By the 1970s, my hometown team, the Pittsburgh Steelers, were dominating the NFL, winning four super bowl titles. Most starters from this decade would amass an unguaranteed salary of around $60,000 per season.

In the 1970s, thanks in large part to the Steelers winning four Super Bowls in a span of six years, none other than Howard Cosell proclaimed Pittsburgh to be "The City of Champions" during a live Monday Night Football broadcast. At that time, the Pittsburgh Steelers still had yet to turn a profit. In fact, it has been reported that the Steelers never earned a profit until 1987 or 1988.

By the 1980s, the owners and the player's union were in regular conflict. There were lockouts and strikes and long periods without a collective bargaining agreement that set forth the rules and regulations between the owners and the players. Most of the problems stemmed from the growing revenue of the league. The compromise ended in the early 1990s, when the salaries of the players grew to new heights, with some superstars now being paid over one million per season and the owner's franchise values growing into the hundreds of millions of dollars.

The players in the 1980s were very fortunate if they were making $100,000 per season. People believe that if you played in the NFL, you are a millionaire. However, in the 1980s, it was the norm for players to make under $100,000 per season. It started to grow slightly above that benchmark as the 1980s progressed and as the sport was growing.

In the late 1980s, my family had the opportunity to pick up two season tickets for seats at Three Rivers Stadium. The Steelers were struggling in those years. Our seats were a couple rows behind the visitor's bench on the forty-five-yard line. My dad would take turns going to the games with each of us. Typically, Monday nights were for him and my mom. The rest of the Sundays were split between my brother and me. I made sure that I got to see some of my favorite teams including the Giants, Oilers, and 49ers. As a ten-to-fourteen-year-old, it was really nice to sit up close to the players. In that old stadium, your view was typically of the back of the jerseys of the players.

I recall going to the games and taking pictures. Many of those pictures, years later, turned out to be guys who I represent in the NFL Concussion Case.

Meanwhile, the league continued to grow in stature. It wins every legal battle. It kept their anti-trust exemption in court. This means that they have little to no regulations that require them to follow the country's laws for fair practice and business dealings. They also prevail nearly every time taken to the mat on any legal dispute by their players or third parties, arguing that they collectively bargained for their rights.

The NFL is a 501(c)6. They are a non-profit association that has large tax benefits as long as they continue to net their profits to zero. They are able to do that by paying executives, lawyers, and a commissioner, for instance, $40-plus-million-dollar salaries annually.

Stadiums continue to be built for billions of dollars, paid in part by taxpayers, and individual franchises cost well over a billion dollars to purchase today. The star players are signing contracts for over one hundred million dollars. The average rookie signs a contract well into the hundreds of thousands of dollars. The NFL doesn't just desire to remain the number one game in the United States; however, as the past several years have demonstrated, the NFL dearly wants to expand its global reach staging numerous games in foreign countries such as Mexico, Japan, and London.

CHAPTER 8

Next Asbestos Case—
Mind Wandering

I was wrong in fact very wrong that I would never hear again from Bennet Omalu and his issues surrounding his CTE diagnosis in the four former players. Rather, the very next day after my talk with Dr. Omalu in my office, former players, their friends, their wives and, in some instances, their widows, were lining up to speak with me.

They could not wait to share their life's experiences with someone who would listen. They had nowhere to turn, no one to help. It was as if I was their therapist and they were ready to spill everything to me. They did not show up to speak with me to discuss suing anyone. They just wanted some reassurance that their lives were not normal.

I was instantly stunned by their stories. I could not believe the stories I was hearing about their behaviors. I could not believe their bizarre impulses, anxiety, paranoia, memory loss, and depression. Not only was every story the same, but each one was worse than the last.

It was described to me that the player's life was like throwing a stone in the water. At some point, the ripples from their actions affect everyone, but the player is last one to realize it.

Bennet could not have made up this diagnosis. It was obvious that these guys needed help. After leaving the NFL, many players were left with nearly nothing. Unless they played four seasons in the NFL, they did not get a pension. In other words, they were not vested per the league's definition. If they did get beat up for at least four seasons, their pensions were poverty level at best. By example, for someone that played in the 1970s and 1980s, they earn $250 for every season they played, assuming they played at least four seasons. Therefore, if you were vested, that means you played four years in the league, and you would earn $1,000 per month in pension. The average former player lives off of $12,000 per year. On top of that, they had no healthcare or health insurance.

As background, the NFL Players Association, the union created to protect the rights of the players, always followed a mantra of money now since the days of former NFLPA President Gene Upshaw. This ideology meant that, first and foremost, the union is almost exclusively dedicated toward actions that financially benefit active players, freeing the NFL from having to contribute anything of significance to costly defined benefit pension plans, disability plans, or the like that would benefit the retired player.

On the other hand, most other professional sports organizations take care of their retired players. By example, Major League Baseball's pensions are at maximum levels. If a player participated in one single Major League Baseball game, that individual could qualify for life-time disability benefits.

Most former NFL players never saw a doctor in their life. Those who could afford to see a doctor were largely addicted to painkillers for their joint and bone problems. However, rarely, if ever, did a single one of them see any neuro-specialists or psychiatrists. No one was on any anti-depressant medicine.

When I first spoke to these former NFL professional athletes, I was star struck. I couldn't believe that I, who was hardly thirty years old, was sitting across my office desk and talking to former players who I watched religiously on Sundays. I knew their names, numbers, and their career statistics. I was amazed that they actually wanted to spend time talking to me about their private lives.

I had to draw a line in the sand. I could not be their fan. They were meeting with me to determine whether there was legally anything I could direct them to that could provide them some relief. I have to admit that it was still extremely difficult to sit across from them and not ask for a picture or an autograph.

I left these separate encounters with a story to share with my family. I would call my mom, dad, and brother and say, "I was meeting with a former NFL player today. You remember him?" It was the highlight of my day to share with my family our past love of football becoming my present work experiences.

In the meantime, I was still handling my asbestos caseload. I had one case in particular that I was working on at that time involving a former J&L Steel Pittsburgh employee. He worked as a bricklayer in the Open Hearth. It was a department that used furnaces to heat and make molten steel at temperatures reaching 2,300 degrees Fahrenheit. It was yet another sad case of a true steel worker. He was dying from mesothelioma. This was the incurable asbestos cancer caused solely from asbestos exposure. The cancer causes the lung to be engulfed by a tumor, which has the ultimate effect of causing the victim to suffocate to death.

I recall meeting with the wife and sick husband, discussing the ultimate expected course of his disease early in my representation of them. I recall how this situation once again involved another family member, this time the wife, who was in denial about what I was explaining about her husband and his disease. I insisted that I was not a doctor, and I could be wrong, and his chemotherapy could work and he could out live his eleven-month expectancy. I still knew that I was correct and he would not be around much longer. Therefore, I advised them that they should stick to my legal advice and strategy on how to handle the case.

I knew that I had to complete his deposition. A deposition is a question-and-answer session with a court reporter who makes a transcript where the parties who are sued get to ask questions to my client under oath. Without his deposition testimony, I would be stuck searching for former co-workers to be his eyes and ears from a time period of forty to fifty years ago. There were not many of those former employees who were still living and could remember my client from that far back.

After finally convincing the wife that we needed to move quickly, despite her objections and complaints, we secured a date in the upcoming week. Because of the amount of information that we would need to discuss, I knew that I had to spend two or three sessions with him preparing him for all the questions. I knew that I would have to test his memory to recall a long time ago in his life when he was more concerned about collecting a paycheck as opposed to concentrating on what was going on around him.

We did the deposition in a conference room of a hotel within minutes from his home. By the time the deposition was scheduled, he was already medically about six months post diagnosis of his illness. He was already going downhill very rapidly. His stamina was very poor. He couldn't handle more than an hour or two without needing rest.

The deposition took a couple of days to complete. We even had to move the final sessions to their family home because the five-minute drive to the hotel was hurting his ability to complete the deposition.

By the end of the deposition, the wife was furious with me. She wouldn't even speak to me. She didn't understand why I had to ask him about his life, his marriage, and his thoughts about losing his family. I guess I didn't even notice much of this while it was happening. I was focused on his testimony and making sure that I could get the best possible financial recovery for them. I also think that I didn't notice her attitude toward me, because I was having a difficult time focusing after meeting with those NFL players and their loved ones. I could not get over the stories that I was told concerning their cognitive and behavioral problems.

I had been losing sleep over what could be done for them. I recall Bennet telling me about Bob Fitzsimmons's case against the NFL disability plan on behalf of Mike Webster's family. I was not interested in going after a disability plan problem. I don't believe that it is worth fighting city hall for one guy. Sure, you may win the occasional battle, but ultimately, the league controls the disability plan, so if you win, they will just make a change to the provisions in the plan, and you won't win against them the next time.

My thoughts were growing. I was concerned that the brain damage was not just a random player or two. It seemed like every former player, or at least everyone I spoke with, had these common problems. They all needed help with their brain injuries. Why was the NFL not helping them? Why was the NFL attempting to discredit Dr. Omalu?

I believed that I was on to something big in the legal world. I believed this called for an investigation. It required searching, asking questions, studying the law, and becoming the expert on the issue.

How was I going to do that? I just turned thirty. I was doing fine at my job. I was moving up the ladder at my law firm with my success on my client's cases. I wasn't causing any problems. I was on the right path for my career choice. How would I find the time to figure out the legalities of this issue? What would my firm say? I knew that I had to keep it quiet at first and look at some of these issues with every extra second I had.

CHAPTER 9

Exploring Case

There really isn't extra time in the practice of law, especially if you are a good lawyer. You don't have extra time to search for new ideas and areas of business. Your time as a civil trial lawyer is mainly devoted to working up cases that have established merit and the client has sustained a significant injury. Remember that the business model of the personal injury lawyer is that we don't get paid unless our clients get paid. You don't want to spend time on unknown matters, because every minute spent is less time to quickly get to those existing cases that have known and expected monetary gain. Further, there is the old philosophy that you could waste your time on the bad cases. The old saying in the profession is that lawyers spend 90 percent of their time on the bad cases and 10 percent of their time on the good cases. We all needed to avoid those bad cases that bog down your time.

I, however, was determined to find time to explore the NFL issue. I needed to call back to Bennet to discuss the medicine and science. I needed to talk with him about concussions and how they happen.

I called Bennet and told him that I was intrigued by this issue. I wanted to investigate it further. Bennet was thrilled to receive this call. I think he was excited, like the players, to have someone that believed him. He was more than happy to introduce me to people who had experience and training in concussion diagnoses and care. In the meantime, he suggested that I read Chris Nowinski's book called *Head Games*.

I spent the next few days taking all of my spare time reading the book. It was an eye-popping series of interviews revolving around concussions in the NFL. There were many players who he interviewed who were battling the same demons after their retirement to the retired players and families with whom I recently spoke. They were struggling with the same depression, memory loss, anxiety, and erratic behavioral issues that were told to me.

Chris did a good job of analyzing the game of football in comparison to science and physics. Chris interviewed the players and asked them about their playing days. How many games did they miss due to concussions? How many times had the player been knocked out? Seen stars? Experienced confusion?

He talked about Merril Hoge. He was a former Pittsburgh Steeler running back who then moved onto to the Chicago Bears, playing eight seasons in the NFL and drafted in the tenth round out of Idaho State. During his last season with the Chicago Bears, Hoge sustained a concussion and was released by the Bear's team physician to play five days later over a telephone call without physically examining him to return to play. Hoge then suffered yet another serious concussion during that game.

He ultimately went to see Dr. Joseph Maroon, the same guy who criticized Dr. Omalu. He was the Pittsburgh Steeler's team physician at the time. Dr. Maroon diagnosed Merril Hoge with severe memory loss, confusion, and headaches. He warned Merril Hoge that future playing football would cause him to be at a risk of permanent brain injury. So Merril Hoge was forced into an early retirement. Merril Hoge later brought a lawsuit against the team physician of the Chicago Bears for improper handling of his concussion, which forced him into an immediate retirement. Had his concussion been treated properly, he would have still been able to play once he healed. Therefore, Merril Hoge was able to file a lawsuit against the doctor for medical malpractice for not giving him appropriate medical advice about his brain injury, and a jury ultimately awarded him in excess of one million dollars, which was less than the remaining value of his contract.

I also learned of the stories of Steve Young and Troy Aikman. They were two of the best quarterbacks from the decade of the late 1980s and early 1990s. They both had their careers ended by post-concussion syndrome. In the NFC championship game in 1994, Troy Aikman sustained a concussion that caused him to be hospitalized, and he could not even recall the game or who won it.

I studied what a concussion is and how it occurs. A concussion is a sudden acceleration or deceleration that causes a person to have any of the following symptoms: seeing stars, unconsciousness, irritability, loss of memory, confusion, and the list continued. I was stunned that the definition did not say that a person must have all of those symptoms. It said that they could suffer any of those symptoms.

Chris's book then talked about a condition in younger children with developing necks and brains. It was called the second-impact syndrome. It is a serious and sometimes fatal condition linked to not letting your brain recover after a first concussion and then sustaining a second concussion.

He talked of Zack Lystedt. He was a young eleven-year-old who sustained a catastrophic brain injury while playing a school football game. He was placed on a ventilator, he couldn't speak for nine months, it took him thirteen months to get rid of his feeding tube, and he could barely stand on his own. Because of Zack Lystedt, the state of Washington passed legislation to adopt a safety in Youth Sports Act to properly treat and care for concussions. These laws require training and certification of coaches and trainers in concussion identification and removal from games after a suspected concussion. Today, almost every state in the country has adopted similar state laws.

I was stunned with the information. Seeing stars equals a concussion. Second-impact syndrome. More former players with brain injuries. A state government changing their law to protect children after suffering concussions. Certainly, the NFL must have been doing something about this growing problem.

Dr. Bennet Omalu next introduced me to some of the scientists and doctors who were intimately involved with concussions in sports. I spoke with Dr. Robert Cantu and Dr. Julian Bailes during this period of time. They both confirmed to me that concussions are a problem in football. They also confirmed that they stood by Dr. Omalu's diagnosis of CTE. This was especially important that Dr. Cantu agreed with this finding.

By background, Dr. Cantu had published guidelines classifying the extent of a concussion back in 1986. He had a resume with dozens of pages that covered his accolades alone in the medical profession. Dr. Cantu's concussion guidelines largely involved grading the severity of a concussion based on the length of time the person was without consciousness.

It was then that I learned that this was not just a case about concussions. It was also about sub-concussions. Those sub-concussive blows involving the head may not manifest any immediate symptoms and signs that are diagnostic of a concussion. For every one documented concussion, there may be tens to hundreds of sub-concussions. Hundreds to thousands of sub-concussions can equally result in permanent damage to the brain cells on the cellular level resulting in a cumulative effect causing CTE. This, I was certain, concerned the NFL the most. They knew that the game could not be played without players regularly experiencing sub-concussive forces to the head.

Dr. Julian Bailes was a one-time Pittsburgh Steelers team doctor. At the time we spoke, around 2007, he was the chairman of neurosurgery departments at the West Virginia University Hospitals. He came out to defend Dr. Omalu's findings as well. Dr. Bailes even recalled briefing the NFL on Dr. Omalu's findings as an invited guest at a conference. Dr. Bailes was quoted as saying, "The Committee got mad... We got into it. And I'm thinking, 'This is a...disease in America's most popular sport, and how are its leaders responding? Alienate the scientist who found it? Refuse to accept the science coming from him?'"

I was blown away by three people that I came in contact with: Chris Nowinski, Dr. Bailes, and Dr. Cantu. It seemed unquestioned that science and medicine showed a distinct chronic brain illness in the former football players.

I couldn't believe what my investigation had revealed. I went back over Chris's book and all of my conversations. I wrote down specific notes on legal tablets. I went back over all my notes and typed them up. Maybe it was just my way of processing all of this information. But what was next?

I needed to explore the medicine further. I needed to understand what was available and known in the medical community. First, I wanted to learn as much as I could about a concussion as described in the medical dictionaries and journals.

I learned that a concussion was the sudden acceleration or deceleration of the brain that caused tearing. It did not require a loss of consciousness. It did not require a hit to the head. In fact, concussions were most common in falls of the elderly or car crashes with or without hitting of a person's head. I was shocked to learn that concussions have been historically documented for over 2,000 years.

I dug further and deeper to find out the state of the art. This is the idea of who knew what and when they knew it. In the asbestos world, this is the examination of the history of asbestos surrounding what was known, when it was known, and who knew it. The asbestos industry may be more egregious than the tobacco industry when it comes to the state of the art. In the 1940s, there was an unquestionable link between asbestos exposure and it causing tumors and asbestos scaring of the lungs. The asbestos manufacturers not only ignored this, but they paid to conspire and cover up these critical public health concerns showing asbestos caused cancer. By the 1950s, there was a disease associated with asbestos called mesothelioma. By the 1970s, the government stepped in to regulate asbestos exposure. However, companies continued to make asbestos well into the 1980s and it wasn't until kids were dying from schools filled with asbestos that it became a public health crisis. Ironically, despite government intervention, a media firestorm, unions complaining, none of that did the trick to end asbestos exposures. It was the lawsuits that changed everything for the asbestos world. The lawsuits were the equalizer to the companies who disregarded human health and safety. My firm of Goldberg, Perky & White was one of the pioneering law firms of that effort.

There is an entire plethora of medical literature that is easily researched to determine publications on any medical issue you are interested in studying. I therefore went to conduct a medical search surrounding concussions and brain trauma. What I found next was absolutely shocking.

I found that boxers were linked to dementia pugilistica dating to 1928. This is the punch-drunk syndrome causing dementia in boxers. In 1966, there were articles on concussion amnesia published in major credible medical journals such as *Neurology*. By the early to mid-1970s, there were a number of articles published establishing a delayed recovery of a person after concussion and the cumulative effect of concussions on people published in the *Lancet*. This was England's major medical publication just like the New England Journal of Medicine is to the United States. At the same time, there was the introduction of the second-impact syndrome. This was the very serious condition associated with receiving a concussion prior to healing of the initial concussion.

By the 1980s, the literature grew by tenfold. There were multiple references of sports and concussion. Dr. Cantu released his concussion guidelines. There were publications of soccer and football concussions. The literature was growing as it involved boxer's dementia. And curiously, Dr. Maroon, the Pittsburgh Steeler neurosurgeon, was publishing on "Football Head and Neck Injuries" in 1980.

Then I found my first smoking gun. I found a 1952 article published in the New England Journal of Medicine explaining the three-strike rule in football stating that if a person has three concussions, then they must retire or quit the game of football. This was dating back to 1945. This published article was written by the NCAA's safety and health expert, who was affiliated with Harvard and known as the father of sports medicine.

Even though the article wasn't specific to the NFL, I could not believe it. In our country's most prestigious medical journal, there was an article that stated that three concussions end a person's football career. I had to call Bennet and report everything I had learned.

I called Bennet on his cellphone and told him about the former players retiring from concussions. I told him about the Merril Hoge, my conversation with Dr. Bailes and Dr. Cantu, and the smoking gun article in the New England Journal of Medicine. He giggled again and said, "Jason, I told you that you are a good lawyer and would figure this out."

I once again shook my head in disbelief. This guy needed his head checked. What didn't he get? I just told him that I have some ammunition to vindicate him from the NFL's attacks. I said to him, "Bennet, don't you get it? This is why they are attacking your credibility."

Then he said, "Jason, God fights my battles. They can't hurt me because the truth will prevail."

We bid each other a good day, and I told him I would be back to him soon after I did more investigation.

CHAPTER 10

The Players and Their Wives

I was ready to go back to the players and their families. I had so many questions to ask them. I was curious what they were told by the NFL about head trauma. I wondered what the language of their player contracts said about injuries, specifically those concerning concussions. I wondered how they were treated when they showed signs of concussions by the medical staff and trainers.

I started calling and interviewing the former players and their families. I was blown away by what I learned this time. I asked them if they ever saw stars or bright lights while playing. Everyone one of them laughed at me. They all told me that it was part of the game. That type of concussion happened all the time, even during practices. Some told me that they were told by their coaches that they were not hitting hard enough if they didn't see stars.

I asked them how many times they suffered confusion or loss of memory while playing. Again, their responses were unanimous. They all explained that was a regular occurrence during the course of a season. Their teammates would help each other out to remind them of their next play to help them get over these temporary bouts of amnesia. They explained it was common to help another teammate out who was experiencing those symptoms during the course of a game.

I then inquired as to how many of them lost consciousness. I was told that happened quite frequently. Some reported three episodes. Others reported dozens of times during their career. I assumed that they would miss considerable time for these occasions. They again looked at me as if I was from another planet. They told me that they were given smelling salts to alert them to time and place, and then they were asked by the trainer how many fingers were being held up. Regardless if they answered correctly, most did, because the answer was always three, and then they returned to the same game.

I then asked the ultimate question as to whether they were ever on the injury report for a concussion. I asked if they were ever officially told that they had a concussion as a diagnosis. They all explained that they were never advised that a concussion was an injury. It was not even a word they heard used by the medical staff. They were given opioids to get rid of the pain and headaches. They were never told that you had a concussion or it was a problem. Rather, they were told that the player "got his bell rung." It was never reported on a team injury report.

I was amazed. I figured there had to be something more to it. It had to be in their player contracts. I started asking the guys for copies of their contracts. I wanted to read all the fine print to see if the devil was in the details.

I read through numerous contracts that I could get my hands on, and I was amazed that every contract failed to say anything about injuries other than you should not do any activity off the field that caused an injury. If a player got hurt in an offseason activity, the teams didn't owe them anything. Then, of course, there was also the language that none of their contracts were guaranteed.

I went back to the former players. I was adamant that there was something they were not telling me. I asked again about the training staff and team physicians. I wanted to know what was done with them when they obviously had a head injury that caused them to black out, have headaches, or lose memory of the games. They explained that it was simply treated as part of playing football. All players are taught to just deal with the pain. A player never wanted to be in the training room. A player could not miss time or there was someone who was ready to take your spot on the field.

I went to the wives and family members to ask their recollection of the players head injuries. They told me that headaches were almost a daily occurrence. It was just part of the game. Without the headache, they would assume it was a day their husband did not practice. The players always complained of head, neck, and body pain.

In civil injury lawsuits, there is a defense that is regularly raised by companies that are sued. It is called assumption of the risk. The law of assumption of the risk bars or reduces a plaintiff's right to recovery against a negligent defendant if the defendant can demonstrate that the plaintiff voluntarily and knowingly assumed the risks at issue inherent to the dangerous activity in which he was participating at the time. A good example is the vacationer who hires a company to take him scuba diving in an ocean filled with sharks, knowing that the waters would be filled with hungry sharks. I always explain it to my client that if you know something is bad for you and you expose yourself to it, your injury is your own fault.

I completely expected the NFL to attempt this argument as a defense to any head injury cases. I was interested in the players' responses when I asked this question directly. I wanted to see how they would handle this difficult issue. After all, I'm sure the public would come out on the NFL's corner, saying that anyone who hits their head would know that it is bad for you.

I recall asking this question to all of the players. I was blown away by their consistent responses that they didn't know that it could cause these long-term problems they face today. My favorite response was from Leonard Marshall. Leonard has become one of my closest friends throughout this long ordeal. He has a charisma about him that attracts everyone to him. Back in the day, he played eleven seasons in the NFL, mostly with the New York Giants. He captured two super bowl trophies and was voted to the pro-bowl on three occasions.

Leonard was a giant of a man, no pun intended. He stood 6'3" and weighed well over 300 pounds. He tallied over eighty-three career sacks. He played in a 3-4 defense that required three down linemen to take on multiple offensive lineman so that the four linebackers could make the plays. Leonard was on the same side of the defense as the greatest outside linebacker of all time, Lawrence Taylor. He became known as "LT" because Leonard Marshall was able to open up so much space for LT to become the NFL's greatest linebacker and defensive player of all time.

After football, Leonard was successful in his many endeavors because of his business sense and ability to network with everyone he met. He always remembered something about everyone who he met and would immediately keep track of their contact information. Leonard was also a great speaker. This led him to teaching a class at Seton Hall University near his home in New Jersey on finances and sports management.

When posed the question concerning assumption of the risk to Leonard in one of his first public interviews, I knew that the NFL would never succeed on this defense. Leonard explained that "he knew the playing football would cause broken bones, hurt knees, chronic joint problems. Hell, you could even become paralyzed, but no one knew that, years later, we would have chronic brain damage that would affect our lives and require us to need help with our simple tasks like going to the store or, in the more serious cases, requiring skilled care for our dementia and depression."

Leonard Marshall was one of the original voices of this concussion issue and advocate on behalf of the plight of the former brain-damaged NFL player. He has taken it upon himself to create a non-profit called "The Gameplan Foundation" that provides help for retired players in need of assistance. He is no different than other players as he also suffers those same problems and often struggles to get out of bed to start his day.

At this point in time, I felt certain that we had enough facts in our favor as to how the National Football League operated and failed to help those who suffer concussions. It was time to give Bennet another phone call to let him know what I learned, but before I did that, I wanted to research whether the NFL had ever been sued in a similar situation.

CHAPTER 11

Learning the Law

My least favorite task as a lawyer is researching case law. It is a tedious but necessary function of the legal analysis. It requires researching decades of statutes and case law trying to find cases that are similar to the case on which you are working. Ultimately, there are two ways to do legal research, either through using one of the legal online directories that provide past case law and statutes across the country. The other method is doing an internet search. I chose the latter as any cases against the NFL would definitely be public record.

I figured that searching the internet would also provide for media commentary on the NFL. After all, my guess was that the NFL probably couldn't get sued without getting some media attention.

I asked one of the young attorneys to provide me a list of cases where the NFL was sued. Surprisingly, the NFL was sued many times between 1976 to the present. I was provided a list of thirty-five cases that involved judicial decisions. Of those thirty-five cases, there were really on three of them that were helpful to provide some useful legal guidance.

In the practice of law, a case becomes binding if an appellate court rules on the matter in the same jurisdiction or court system. In that situation, the trial court must follow that decision as being the law on the subject or issue. The chances of finding an identical or similar fact pattern involving the NFL would be slim to none. However, on the other hand, I was optimistic that I could find some persuasive authority involving the NFL. A case becomes persuasive if it involves a relatively similar issue that was decided in some other court system. In that situation, the trial judge does not have to follow that law; however, he or she could rely upon it because it provides an analysis of a similar issue albeit from applying another state's laws.

The first case that I came across involved the Estate of Korey Stringer versus the NFL and Riddell. Korey Stringer was six feet and four inches tall and weighed 340-plus pounds. He played offensive tackle and was drafted out of Ohio State University in the first round, pick twenty-four. He played from 1995 to 2000 with the Minnesota Vikings, reaching the pro-bowl in his last full season. He played in ninety-three games in his career and started ninety-one of them.

The Minnesota Vikings preseason training camp was held at a practice facility in Mankato, Minnesota. Korey Stringer, who weighed 335 pounds, vomited three times during the morning conditioning drills in stifling humidity and temperatures in the low nineties. A trainer was not summoned until after all the drills had ended.

Korey Stringer then went to an air-conditioned trailer serving as a training room on the practice field and lost consciousness at the preseason practice facility which was located at Minnesota State University. Paramedics were called to the scene, and he was rushed to Immanuel St. Joseph's-Mayo Health Center. It was reported that his body temperature was 108.8. His organs failed, and he never regained consciousness before dying at 1:50 a.m. the next morning.

Korey Stringer had struggled with weight problems early in his career before slimming down. He reported to camp at 335 pounds and was in the best shape of his career. Nevertheless, he reportedly struggled the first day of camp, when he was taken off the practice field on a cart.

Korey, who was twenty-seven at the time, was survived by his wife, Kelci, and a three-year-old son, Kodie. A wrongful death lawsuit was filed on Korey's behalf in federal court in the Southern District of Ohio. The lawsuit alleged that the NFL had a duty to use ordinary care in overseeing, controlling, and regulating the member clubs' practices, policies, procedures, equipment, working conditions, and culture insofar as they pertain to and subject players to heat-related illness, including, but not limited to, the duty to institute acclimatization requirements and to regulate training camp practices, other practices, games, equipment, and medical care so as to minimize the risk of heat-related illness.

The NFL denied these claims and filed a motion to dismiss on the basis that plaintiff's claims were preempted by Section 301 of the Labor Management Relations Act, 29 USC § 185. The National Football League repeatedly relied on this statute as a shield to protect them from all lawsuits. Their argument was that in order to resolve this legal claim, the NFL's collective bargaining agreement would need to be interpreted.

The Estate of Korey Stringer answered the NFL's motion by explaining that the collective bargaining agreement or CBA would not have to be interpreted, and the duty breached was a duty that arose from state tort or civil law. The Stringers contended that interpretation of the CBA was unnecessary because the duty that the NFL breached was a "common-law duty of care [and] is that degree of care which an ordinarily reasonable and prudent person exercises, or is accustomed to exercising, under the same or similar circumstances."

This was the first time that I had come across this reference to labor preemption and section 301 of the Labor Management Relations Act. This was not a hot ticket item that was discussed much, if at all, in law school in core classes. The National Labor Relations Act of 1935 is a statute of labor law which provides for basic rights of private employees to organize into unions, engage in collective bargaining for better terms and conditions at work, and strike if necessary.

Founded in 1956, the NFL's union, known as the National Football League Players' Association, was established to provide players with formal representation to negotiate compensation and the terms of their collective bargaining agreement.

In the early years of the NFL, contractual negotiations took place between individual players and management as team owners were reluctant to engage in collective bargaining. Over the years, a number of strikes and lockouts occurred in the NFL due to monetary and benefit disputes between the players and the owners. League rules that punished players for playing in rival football leagues resulted in litigation. This resulted in the NFL being compelled to negotiate some work rules and minimum payments with the NFL Players' Association. However, the organization was not recognized by the NFL as the official bargaining agent for the players until 1968, when a CBA was signed. The most recent CBA negotiations took place in 2011.

In addition to conducting labor negotiations, the NFL Players' Association represents and protects the rights of the players. For instance, they are involved in filing grievances against player discipline that it deems too severe. The union also ensures that the terms of the collective bargaining agreement are adhered to by the league and the teams. NFL players' union negotiates and monitors retirement and insurance benefits for active players and enhances and defends the image of players and their profession.

The Supreme Court of the United States has often resolved issues involving labor preemption. They have routinely defined our country's laws surrounding collective bargaining agreements between employers and employees in disputes. The law can be summed up as stating that anytime the collective bargaining agreement needs consulted, then it is a matter that is inappropriate for the courts to decide and, therefore, the dispute is preempted, typically requiring contractual or CBA resolution. In the case of most collective bargaining agreements, this means that the only recourse of the employee is to file a grievance on behalf of his union.

In the Stringer lawsuit, the trial court, in large part, dismissed the NFL from the case finding that the collective bargaining agreement needed to be interpreted to determine the rules and regulations concerning practicing in high heat. However, the appellate court on appeal found that "Plaintiff's (Stringer's) claim does not arise out of the CBA. Neither the NFL nor NFL Properties is a party to the CBA. While both Defendants are mentioned in the CBA, the CBA imposes no duty on either of them to ensure that the equipment used by NFL players adequately protects from risk of injury or illness. And such duty, if it exists, clearly has its course in the common law."

NFL Properties is the licensing arm of the NFL. They are a subsidiary of the NFL that is responsible for licensing the equipment that the players use. Since they were not a party involved in the negotiations of the collective bargaining agreement, they were not afforded the same protection as the NFL. There was no contractual dispute between Korey Stringer and NFL Properties.

The Stringers also sued Riddell for negligence, or failing to meet their legal duty of providing an adequate warning when practicing in high temperatures while wearing their officially NFL licensed pads and helmets. The court found that "there is no evidence in the record that Stringer had any knowledge of the heightened risk of developing heat stroke, as opposed to the general risk of becoming hotter, associated with wearing Defendants' helmet and shoulder pads in the extremely hot and humid conditions of the Vikings' training camp. Additionally, the question of whether a user's knowledge of the risks posed by a product will excuse the manufacturer's duty to warn is generally a question of fact that is not properly resolved on summary judgment. The Court concludes that the risk was not obvious."

Ultimately, the Stringers entered separate confidential settlements with the NFL, NFL Properties, and Riddell. It was rumored that the settlement was in the tens of millions of dollars. As part of that settlement, the only disclosed term was that the NFL will support efforts to create a heat illness prevention program. Many professional football teams now train in light color uniforms, water and shade are made readily available, and a team doctor is at practice sessions at all times.

Interestingly, during the course of discovery in the Stringer case, it was uncovered that the NFL provided paperwork on practicing in high heat to all teams and their players. They, in essence, undertook a duty to provide insight and higher knowledge of this issue.

The second case that intrigued me involved another offensive lineman by the name of Orlando Brown. Orlando "Zeus" Brown was a huge offensive tackle who played nearly ten seasons in the NFL with the Cleveland Browns and Baltimore Ravens. He was six fee and seven inches tall and weighed around 360 pounds. He was, at one time, the highest paid offensive lineman in football and finished his career having played 129 career games.

In 1999, Orlando Brown was hit directly in the right eye by a penalty flag which was weighted with ball bearings thrown by the referee. The referee, Jeff Triplette, immediately apologized to Brown during the game. Orlando Brown was holding his hand to his eye and then went ballistic and shoved Triplette to the ground. Brown was ejected from the game and subsequently suspended by the NFL, although the suspension was lifted when his injury did not heal.

Orlando Brown sat out the entire 2000 regular season hoping his eye would heal. When it did not heal, he sued the NFL for $200 million in damages. According to rumors, he reportedly settled for a sum between $15 million and $25 million in 2002.

In 2001, Brown filed suit against the NFL seeking damages for the NFL's negligence. The NFL claimed that Orlando Brown's claim was governed by the CBA and should be sent to arbitration. The federal court in the Southern District of New York disagreed.

> It does not follow, however, that any state tort suit brought by an employee covered by a CBA is preempted by the LMRA. Federal preemption is driven by the need to ensure "that the meaning given a contract phrase or term be subject to uniform federal interpretation. Thus, questions relating to what the parties to a labor agreement agreed, and what legal consequences were intended to flow from breaches of that agreement, must be resolved by reference to uniform federal law, whether such questions arise in the context of a suit for breach of contract or in a suit alleging liability in tort.
>
> Tort claims that do not implicate these federal interests are not preempted. The test is whether the tort claim is "inextricably intertwined with consideration of the terms of the labor contract.
>
> Plaintiffs' theory of the case is that this is a garden-variety tort action invoking a general duty to avoid negligently causing harm, owed by

the NFL not only to its players but also to any other person in society who could possibly have been threatened by Triplette's weighted projectile. They contend that a fan, member of the press, or other bystander could equally bring such a claim had he or she been injured in the same manner. On this view, whether Triplette or the NFL was negligent, or whether the NFL has a valid defense that Brown assumed the risk of such an injury by playing professional football (or any other defense to the action), are simply ordinary issues of state tort law that, in the absence of diversity of citizenship, should be adjudicated in state court.

In this case, however, the duty asserted by Brown is based on state tort law, and would protect any member of the public. The NFL owes no greater duty to Brown than to any bystander (and Brown does not claim that it does) to train its employees in the safe use of their equipment or to respond in damages if one of its employees in the course of his work carelessly throws something into someone's eye.

This provided an instance of showing that the NFL is not protected by the collective bargaining agreement when there is an issue that is not founded in a contract dispute. This issue of throwing an object was well outside the ordinary circumstances that the NFL and the NFL Players' Association could have ever discussed or negotiated during their contractual bargaining session.

I was excited to find a case holding the NFL directly responsible for an active player's injuries. It provided legal authority, albeit persuasive in nature, to help understand that a lawsuit was plausible.

The third case that I came across dealt with the Williams brothers from the Minnesota Vikings. Pat and Kevin Williams were suspended by the NFL for four games after violating the league's drug policy on banned substances. The NFL Players' Association challenged the confirmation of arbitration awards, upholding the play-ers' suspensions for using bumetanide, a banned prescription diuretic contained in a dietary supplement, in violation of a policy incorpo-rated into the collective bargaining agreement. On appeal, the appel-late court in Minnesota agreed that the players' claims under the Minnesota's Drug and Alcohol Testing in the Workplace Act were not preempted by the Labor Management Relations Act as the Williams' alleged the violation of a state law that did not require interpretation of the NFL collective bargaining agreement.

However, the Williams' common law claims were preempted by the Labor Management Relations Act because they were inextricably intertwined with the collective bargaining agreement.

Ultimately, the Williams brothers' suspension of four games was upheld. However, this case provided another thought to suing the NFL. Was there some state law violation that could be alleged as the cause of the player's brain injuries?

By now, I was feeling hopeful. Yes, the NFL typically wins, but they have lost a time or two. Well, at least they were not undefeated. However, there was one thing bothering me about my legal analysis and review of cases. I was still concerned whether a lawsuit would be dismissed from court if the NFL would be considered an employer and, therefore, be immune from a lawsuit due to state workers com-pensation laws. This means that any claim a player would have would be exclusively against his employer, which would be his team who paid his salary, and be capped by the state's workers' compensation laws. Ultimately, this issue was decided by the Supreme Court of the United States of America in a Sherman Act violation case involving the NFL's licensing arrangements with certain apparel manufactur-ers. By 2010, the Supreme Court of the United States ruled in a case brought by American Needle clothing company that the NFL is a separate entity from each of its teams.

My review of legal cases illustrated that I could cite some cases that showed the NFL lost. I felt confident that every lawyer in the country would be excited to hear and get involved in this massive law-suit against the NFL, who may have thirty-two of the deepest pockets in the planet. I could not have been more wrong in my thinking.

CHAPTER 12

The Coverup by the League

My investigation next led me to explore the issue of the NFL's attacks on my friend, Dr. Bennet Omalu. I wanted to understand why they believed Bennet's identification of CTE was wrong. I wanted to know what research they had done into the issue of concussions and long-term brain injury of football players. I wanted to know if the NFL had information that disproved Dr. Omalu's findings and reports. However, what I found harkened the word that I struggled to spell in Elementary school, F-R-A-U-D.

The NFL undertook the responsibility of studying concussion research in 1994 through funding a committee known as the NFL Committee on Mild Traumatic Brain Injury. This came as the result of a number of players who were retiring due to post-concussion syndrome including Troy Aikman, Steve Young, and Al Toon. Al Toon was a standout wide receiver for the New York Jets who suffered at least nine concussions over his eight-year career, forcing him to retire at the age of twenty-nine.

The Mild Traumatic Brain Injury Committee was chaired by Dr. Elliot Pellman, who was a rheumatologist by practice and a New York Jet team physician. He was not trained in brain injuries or any neuro-physician specialties.

In 2006, the NFL's MTBI committee finally published their research involving football players after being in existence for twelve years. Shockingly, the committee reported that the NFL lacked any concussion problems. One paper published in *Neurosurgery* showed that, because a significant percentage of players returned to play the same game after suffering a concussion and they typically were kept out of football for less than one week, they concluded that concussions in professional football are not serious injuries. According to the NFL's committee, the speedy return to play after suffering a concussion demonstrates that such players were not at a greater risk for suffering long-term brain injury.

However, this summary paper on their research and opinions of football players was not the only literature produced by the NFL Mild Traumatic Brain Injury Committee. They regularly contradicted the research and experiences of decades of neurologists and scientists concerning the damage done by concussion in humans.

For example, in a 2004 journal, the MTBI Committee published a paper in which it asserted that the committee's research found no risk of repeated concussions in players with previous concussions and that there was no seven- to ten-day window of increased susceptibility to sustaining another concussion.

As a further example, in January 2004, the committee wrote that returning to play after a concussion "does not involve significant risk of a second injury either in the same game or during the season." This was in direct contrast to a 2003 NCAA study that consisted of 2,900 former college players which found the opposite and related that "those who have suffered concussion are more susceptible to further head trauma for seven to ten days after the injury."

In total, there were sixteen papers published in *Neurosurgery*, which became the NFL's go to medical journal to publish about their lack of a concussion problem. At the head of the *Neurosurgery* journal was Editor Michael Apuzzo. Dr. Apuzzo had a very impressive scholarly past as a neuro-physician. However, he was at the head of the journal and acted to publish as many articles as possible discrediting any problems in the NFL related to head trauma or later life brain injury from playing football. Michael Apuzzo's curious background included being a sideline consultant for the New York Giants.

The journals included papers involving purported studies of reconstruction of game impacts and injuries, helmet impacts, neuropsychological testing, players returning to the game, and repeat injuries to name a few. My personal favorite happened to be the comparison with boxing head impacts. All articles either listed Dr. Casson, Dr. Pellman, or Dr. Viano as the lead writer. These were the heads of the NFL's concussion committee.

In the meantime, Dr. Omalu was determined and working to publish his findings of Mike Webster's CTE. I recall Bennet sharing with me that he went about doing so in the NFL's journal, *Neurosurgery*. He was asked that his original draft be edited to remove a number of suggestions that the NFL knew of brain damage and intentionally ignored it. After all, what does that have to do with science? However, when it was published in July of 2005, he soon received a call asking that his paper be retracted. This was a direct attack on Dr. Omalu's integrity as a physician and scientist. He would need to defend his findings or face ridicule. Of course, the letter challenging Omalu's publication was from none other than doctors Casson, Pellman, and Viano. This was yet another nuclear attack on Dr. Omalu, a foreigner, to discredit him and ruin his career in front of his peers. Bennet remained steadfast through the ordeal. He had science, history, and the actual degenerative brains of the football players on his side.

Dr. Pellman ultimately stepped down as the head of the MTBI Committee in February 2007. Dr. Ira Casson and Dr. David Viano replaced Dr. Pellman as the heads of the MTBI. Dr. Casson became the voice of strong anti-concussion problems in former football players. He, unlike Dr. Pellman, was a neurologist and proudly portrayed himself as a man of science. Both Dr. Casson and Viano continued to dismiss outside studies and overwhelming evidence linking dementia and other cognitive decline to brain injuries. When asked in 2007 whether concussions could lead to brain damage, dementia, or depression, Dr. Casson denied the linkage six separate times in a special interview. He became known as "Dr. No" for his statements that football did not cause any chronic brain damage.

During the same time, the NFL approached Bennet, requesting to perform their own analysis on the tissue slides of the brains of Webster, Long, and Waters. Bennet told me that they brought with them neuro-pathologists to privately review the slides to come to their own conclusions. These doctors specifically hired by the NFL agreed with Dr. Omalu's interpretation that these former players suffered from a new chronic brain disease. However, they never made it known that they agreed that Dr. Omalu had uncovered football's chronic brain injury. Rather, as their letter to *Neurosurgery* stated, the NFL was adamant that they were "not going to bow to some no-name Nigerian with some bullshit theory."

The NFL seemed to have a strong stance opposing this issue of football causing later-life concussion problems. At least there were agents of the NFL actively stating the same despite having concrete proof of the opposite. It was truly troubling as there was no reason to support their conclusion in the scientific and medical community outside of the science they were fabricating. Why were they attempting to attack Bennet's findings? What were they trying to hide?

CHAPTER 13

The NFL Is a Giant

The NFL has proven that their brand is untouchable. I talked at great length of the NFL's almost perfect record in the court system. The NFL also owns a nearly perfect record before its own disability system.

The NFL created a disability system to provide a benefit to those who suffer a football induced or non-football related injury. The Bert Bell NFL Player Retirement Plan has provided disability benefits to eligible professional football players since 1962. The key word being eligible. The Pete Rozelle NFL Player Retirement Plan was established in 1989 to provide benefit accruals from that point forward in a manner similar to the Bert Bell Plan. In 1994, the two plans were merged.

The deciding factor is that the board will be made up of three voting members appointed by the NFL, three members appointed by the NFL Players' Association, and the commissioner is the honorary chairman. In the event of a deadlocked decision, it can go to binding arbitration. The problem is that the system appoints three people from the NFL Players Association who have historically not been a friend of the retired player. As the late former head of the players' association, Gene Upshaw, was famously quoted as saying, "I don't represent the retired players."

The first hurdle to retired players to recover disability benefits is to show that they have four credited seasons in the NFL. A former player gets one credited season for every season that he is on the active list for at least three games.

In the case of one of my original clients in the concussion lawsuit against the NFL, George Visger, he gets nothing. George played less than a handful of games in the 1980 to 1981 season. George was part of the 1981 Super Bowl champion San Francisco 49ers as a defensive lineman. During one game during the Super Bowl season, George suffered a devastating hit that caused him not to recall completing the remainder of the game let alone receiving over twenty smelling salts from the trainer.

Going into his second season, George was injured during training camp. He complained of concussion-like symptoms and was seen by the team physician. After days of complaints and progressively worsening of his condition, he reported back to the team physician, who shined a light in George's eyes to only exclaim, "Your brain is hemorrhaging." George was told to drive home and rest and go later in the day to a doctor's visit arranged by the team physician for George.

George Visger luckily survived to tell his story. However, the damage was done. This incident caused him nine emergency brain surgeries. He has a shunt placed in his head to handle his diagnosis of hydrocephalus, or fluid on the brain. George also has developed dementia. His last twenty years have been covered by yellow tablets that keep track of his daily experiences and conversations though journaling his life.

For his efforts, George was cut by the 49ears while hospitalized, he was given his last rites, he was almost not given his super bowl ring by the 49ers that he earned, and he was left without the ability to even apply for lifetime disability benefits from the NFL. Without George's efforts to fight the team in the workers compensation system and opening his own businesses, George would have been another casualty requiring assistance from one of our government system. Despite being worth billions of dollars, the league refuses to take care of those who are disabled while playing their sport if they did not have a sufficient number of credited seasons.

Some may say, so what? George survived. Life isn't fair. The system says he didn't play enough games. It's a shame he was not a Major League Baseball player. Things would have been different as he would have been vested sooner.

For those skeptics, I think it is necessary to share how the NFL disability system has routinely treated those claims made by the vested players. For those that are successful, they get paid a disability if the six-person board agrees that you have proven that medically you are no longer able to work anywhere for pay. The reality is that there are few successful applications that are approved by the NFL disability system.

Dave Pear's story is a typical example of the NFL's sham of a disability system. Dave Pear was born in Vancouver, Washington, and grew up in Portland, Oregon. Dave attended the University of Washington on an athletic scholarship and played defensive tackle for the Washington Huskies from 1971 to 1974. He was the first Tampa Bay Buccaneers player to ever be selected to a Pro Bowl. He played and won super bowl XV with the Oakland Raiders.

After leaving football with a broken neck after six seasons, Dave has been fighting the NFL for his earned disability and medical benefits since 1979. Since his first application was turned down in 1983, he has become a vocal advocate for the retired players' rights.

Specifically, in 1983, Dave applied for the line of duty benefit from the Bell/Rozelle Disability Plan. In order to receive this benefit, a player's injury had to be caused from football, and an NFL doctor had to rate you at least 50 percent disabled. However, the NFL had the discretion to award or deny the player this benefit. The NFL physician wrote that Dave Pear's neck injury was caused from football, and he checked the box on the form illustrating a 50 to 59 percent disability. Despite this proof, the NFL Disability Board denied the benefit to Dave. In his early thirties, Dave was left in a state of constant and chronic pain in his neck and a growing memory problem and had to seek out employment to provide for his family.

By 1995, Dave tried to reach out the NFL Players Association as the pain in his low back and neck was getting worse requiring more surgery. He was advised that he could apply for total and permanent disability. This would require another visit with an NFL doctor while paying his own travel expenses as well as paying for this doctor's bill of services. Dave was examined by an NFL physician, Dr. Hugh Unger, in Miami. In his report, Dr. Unger wrote, "From my physical examination, this patient is markedly incapacitated from both the cervical and lumbar areas, all of which were secondary to injuries sustained while playing professional football." He then checked the box indicating Dave Pear's disability to be 80 percent or more disabled, which was the highest level on the form. Dr. Unger then stated that Dave was able to engage in sedentary work with no excessive standing, no bending, and no lifting over seven to fifteen pounds. However, he wrote that Dave must be able to rest frequently on the job. Despite the medical documentation as required by the NFL's own doctor to the exact requirements of the disability plan definitions, Dave Pear was again denied his total and permanent benefits.

Dave then called the NFL Players' Association office. He was advised by Miki Yaris Davis, who has served as the senior director of player benefits for over forty years, that there was nothing further that could be done for Dave Pear. Dave inquired whether any other retired players were receiving this benefit and was told by her that the only one she knew of was Daryl Stingly, and he was paralyzed and in a wheelchair. Miki Yarris Davis advised him that unless he was in a wheelchair, then he would not get this NFL benefit.

Dave continued to call his union time and time again asking for help, but their answers were always the same. There was nothing they could do for him.

Dave was not about to let the NFL win this battle. He wanted his grievance heard by the NFL's commissioner. Despite numerous calls to the league office to speak with the commissioner, Roger Goodell finally called him back in 2007. Dave Pear spent almost thirty minutes explaining his difficulties with the disability plan. At the end of our phone call, Dave related that Roger Goodell asked him, "Who do you think I am, God?"

Dave Pear responded, "No, you are the commissioner of the NFL, you have the power to fix this injustice for retired players."

Commissioner Goodell appointed his own attorney, Larry Lamade, to call Dave Pear. Larry has worked for the league for over forty years and is paid by the NFL Players' Association, the NFL, and the NFL's disability plan at the same time. Once again, this shows an extreme conflict of interest between these entities. Larry Lamade told Dave that he was being tasked with offering to be an intermediary. At the time, Dave was trying to get a copy of the plan document from the Bert Bell Rozelle Disability Plan, and the office refused to provide him with a copy. This document is the long, detailed explanation of an employee's benefits but is only given to the employee upon written request. Cynthia Timpson, who works for the plan, once told Dave Pear that they were still working on the plan. When Dave called the plan office and asked for the director, Sarah Gaunt, they would hang the telephone up on him once he provided them with his name.

Four months later, after Larry Lamade was appointed by the commissioner of the NFL to help Dave Pear without any success, Dave received an anonymous threat on his website blog from a Catherine that said, "I would be careful who you arbitrarily and falsely accuse, David." This was traced directly back to Larry Lamade's office.

Let me take the devil's advocate position; maybe the NFL was doing a good job of policing their disability payments so that that they do not pay out money to frivolous claims. After all, what are the chances of a former NFL gladiator hurting his body so badly that he can no longer work any type of job? Not so far-fetched or bold on the part of the league to handle their own former players this way? Certainly, the NFL would not be insincere when called to task before the Congress of the United States of America.

Because of scrutiny and media pressure, the NFL scheduled a league-wide concussion summit for June 2007. At the summit, the co-chair of the NFL's Mild Traumatic Brain Injury Committee, Dr. Ira Casson, told team doctors and trainers that CTE has never been scientifically documented in football players. The NFL issued a pamphlet to players in August 2007, which stated, "There is no magic number for how many concussions is too many." The pamphlet further deceived the league's current players by stating "We want to make sure all NFL players...*are fully informed* and take advantage of the *most up to date information* and resources as we continue to study the long-term impact on concussions." Once again, the NFL failed to acknowledge a horrible problem with football concussions. They failed to at minimum warn those who played the game that there is no safe concussion.

In 2008, the University of Michigan's Institute for Social Research conducted a study on the health of retired players, with over one thousand former NFL players taking part. The results of the study, which were released in 2009, reported that "Alzheimer's disease or similar memory-related diseases appear to have been diagnosed in the league's former players vastly more often than in the national population—including a rate of 19 times the normal rate for men ages 30 through 49." Showing their above the law mentality, the NFL, which had commissioned the study, responded to its results by claiming that the study was incomplete. They relayed that further investigation and facts would be needed to make a firm conclusion.

In October 2009, congressional hearings were held before the United States House Judiciary Committee. Committee member Linda Sanchez analogized the NFL's denial of a causal link between NFL concussion and cognitive decline to the tobacco industry's denial of the link between cigarette consumption and ill health effects.

Also at the October 2009 hearing, Rep. Maxine Waters told the NFL, "I believe you are an $8 billion organization that has failed in your responsibility to the players. We all know it's a dangerous sport. Players are always going to get injured. The only question is, are you going to pay for it? I know that you dearly want to hold on to your profits. I think it's the responsibility of Congress to look at your antitrust exemption and take it away."

NFL Commissioner Roger Goodell testified at the hearing that "[i]n the past 15 years, the NFL has made significant investments in medical and biomechanical research. All of that information has been made public, subjected to thorough and ongoing peer review, published in leading journals, and distributed to the NFLPA and their medical consultants. We have been open and transparent, and have invited dialogue throughout the medical community."

Dr. Casson provided oral and written testimony at the hearings. He continued to deny the validity of other studies, stating that "[t]here is not enough valid, reliable or objective scientific evidence at present to determine whether or not repeat head impacts in professional football result in long term brain damage."

Then Dr. Joe Maroon testified at the congressional hearings. He was the Pittsburgh Steelers' neurosurgeon that was a member of the NFL's Mild Traumatic Brain Injury Committee. He was the first doctor to come out strongly criticizing Dr. Omalu. His statement to Congress said, "Our committee, together with the NFL, has long recognized that concussion can lead to long-term health issues, especially if not properly managed." Did he really say the NFL was aware of health problems from repeated concussions? Then Dr. Maroon stated that players are responsible for reporting their concussions. This was once again laying the responsibility on the person who had just suffered a brain injury and had an impairment of function.

The NFL's power seemed to control science, football and, now, congress. There was no stopping this multibillion dollar giant at this time. Unlike Barry Bonds and other former MLB players who were charged with obstruction of justice and perjury, the NFL walked away from the congressional hearings unscathed. They were even bold enough to state that they have been ahead of the concussion issue. Then they tasked the players with being responsible for reporting their concussions despite their brain dysfunction. All of this information was disappointing to the players suffering from brain injury and the families that were left behind by former deceased players.

CHAPTER 14

The Players Concerns to Sue

Now that the facts and law were coming together for a perfect launch date to file a lawsuit in early 2007, the only thing that I needed to do was sign up brain-injured former players to sue the NFL. This task was much more difficult than you could imagine. There were many factors that were in play as to why this was a problematic decision for players to file a lawsuit against the league that defined their existence.

Another competing interest was the stigma created concerning our American Civil Justice system. There is not a week that passes without me hearing the phrase "tort reform." Tort reform is a disguised form of corporate welfare. It provides protection for corporations in the civil justice system against lawsuits brought by victims. The purpose of tort reform is to limit an injured party's access into court. The other purpose is to cap their financial recovery under the court system. The proponents of tort reform argue that it protects against runaway jury verdicts.

Regardless of what side of the fence you stand on this hot button political issue, the end result has been a chilling effect on the public's mindset. Specifically, there are two engraved biases that have come to the forefront of the public. First, everyone believes that there are too many frivolous lawsuits.

A frivolous lawsuit is one that has no legal basis to be filed in the court system. If a frivolous lawsuit is filed, the legal system offers safeguards like a motion to dismiss or preliminary objections to swiftly remove the case from the court system. I see this issue of jury biases regarding frivolous lawsuits every time I go to jury selection throughout Western Pennsylvania. The voir dire process involves asking jurors questions concerning their ability to be fair and impartial. Voir Dire means to speak the truth. The process is more of a deselection of people who show that they cannot treat your client fairly due to their preconceived opinions and beliefs.

I always ask all jurors in some form or another whether they have any thoughts, opinions, or beliefs about civil damage lawsuits or jury verdicts. Inevitably, over 80 to 90 percent of the thousands of jurors I have asked that question to have answered that questions very strongly against injured persons, citing most commonly the phrases "frivolous lawsuit," "multimillion dollar verdicts," and "McDonald's hot coffee."

Unfortunately, the McDonald's case could not have been further from a frivolous lawsuit. The injured female in that case scalded her private area, requiring surgical revisions despite the numerous documented protests to McDonald's about the extreme temperature of the coffee and how it was burning numerous customers throughout America.

The effect of the tort reform makes it very difficult to convince any person in this day and age that they have a meritorious claim or that they actually had a chance of recovering for their injuries.

The other factor from tort reform has been the increasing distrust in lawyers. Lawyers have reached a new level of disfavor in our society. Recent surveys have shown that lawyers and used car salesmen are running neck and neck as the most distrustful careers by job designation.

Imagine what it is like to meet a new acquaintance for the first time in a social setting. My name is Jason Luckasevic, and I am a lawyer. *Strike one.* I have handled many civil cases like yours. *Strike two.* I have obtained multi-millions of dollars for my clients and my law firm. *Strike three!*

Then apply that same premise to the former NFL athlete. Sprinkle on top of that the fact that I was about to turn a mere thirty-one years old, and my appearance harkened back to the 1990s grunge Generation X of the likes of Nirvana, Everclear, Pearl Jam, and Green Day. I dressed for comfort, not style, and my hair carried a blonde tint over the years. If I were a used car salesman, my chances of selling a vehicle were non-existent with this consumer.

The former players have proven to be my most challenging of clients I have represented in my practice. Just like anything in life, there are strengths and weaknesses that we as lawyers have. I talked about my weakness of researching legal cases earlier. On the other hand, my strength has been my ability to communicate. I am not sure why this, in particular, was my strength. Maybe it was the way that I was raised by my parents that required me to be honest and treat others fairly. Whatever it is, I certainly have an ability to speak to people from any walk of life. I am a compassionate and passionate person. Those characteristics make it easy to relate to others and for them to instantly feel comfortable with me and trusting of my advice and recommendations.

The difference with this class of clients was so much. Maybe it was the fact that we as a society have placed them in at the highest bracket of role models and highest paid persons in our society on average. America idolizes its sports figures. We push our children into sports. Sports have become the go-to profession that our most talented children hope to achieve and parents push their children into.

Because of this, it has led professional athletes to be treated with excessive privileges. It has allowed them access to places that other cannot get into professional sports. It provides them opportunities that others do not have. We seek their autographs and selfies. We want to know them and share in their personal lives in anyway such as following them on social media. We have twenty-four-hour networks covering their careers and lives.

This royal treatment has resulted in the professional athletes being continually taken advantage of in their endeavors. They have had friends and family leech off of their money. They have had investors advise them into spending money on bad deals. Some were pushed into drugs and other criminal activities. More important than anything, they were treated unfairly by lawyers. Their agents took much of their money. Other lawyers created unfair and often non-existent retirement provisions in the collective bargaining agreement. Lastly, the union lawyers did not fight for their rights to provide for them after their playing days were over.

This has resulted in the former NFL players having a supreme distrust for lawyers. They believe that no lawyer cares about their problems. Even recently, the players won a lawsuit for unauthorized use of their images against a sports gaming system. Instead of getting what they were entitled to, the players had to sue those lawyers who represented and won the case for them for legal malpractice for the deal that was largely beneficial to the lawyers and not the players.

Going into my talks with the players and their loved ones, I was not optimistic that they would be enthusiastic of any of this. They also needed to believe in the case. Finally, and most importantly, they needed to believe the end game would be the lawyers looking out to get the players paid and not cut a deal to benefit the lawyers.

To further complicate matters, the former players believed that the league was a reason for their fame. They all, to this very day, love the game of football. Without football, they would not be the men they are today. It was a band of brothers much like the military. To spit at what made you is a taboo idea to this trade. They were taught to be followers, not leaders. Their coaches provided the means and design for their games. They did not need to be free-thinkers. They are reactive by their very nature.

I have heard many a former player questioned about whether they would have played the game again. They have almost unanimously stated that they would have played despite their problems. One of my most famous clients, Tony Dorsett, once talked about it best in a public interview. Tony was one of the most successful running backs in the history of football. He was a Heisman trophy winner in college, and his senior year the team won the national championship. He was drafted as the number two pick in the draft and played a dozen years in the NFL, finishing with one super bowl ring, four all-pros, and later was named a Hall-of-Famer. Tony has given many interviews on head injuries and was one the first NFL Hall-of-Famer's to stand up on this issue and sue the National Football League. He repeatedly stated in interviews that he just wishes that the league would have been upfront with the head injury issue so that the players could make the right decisions about playing and treatment. It wasn't fair for the league to play God with their brains.

I also knew that having only one guy suing the league would not be enough. There needed to be multiple players suing the league for their injuries. I was confident that once we had a sizeable group, others would later join. Thus, I was off to speak with them about the law and the facts.

In my conversations, they hit me with many questions. I was able to handle those difficult questions about lawyers. I took numerous questions about the law. I told them about the NFL's despicable actions, lying about the dangerous outcomes that await the players later in life. Then I explained that this was not about me. I was willing to take a risk because it was the right thing to do to defend the reputation of my friend. I explained to them that I too was taking a risk. My wife, Kelly, was very concerned about this case. A case like this could ruin my career. It could become a money pit. The public could come out strongly against the players. I didn't know better. I was young. I was doing what a lawyer should be doing—protecting those that were hurt wrongly by another.

By the end of the conversations, they believed in me. They were ready to take this fight to court. I had a number of them that were united and ready to file a lawsuit against the NFL in 2007.

CHAPTER 15

The Talk with My Law Firm

The hardest thing in the practice of law is finding clients. I was taught that there are three types of lawyers. First, there are those who find the coin. Second, there are those who polish the coin. Finally, there are those lawyers who turn it into gold.

Ron Motely was one of the best civil trial lawyers and practiced out of South Carolina. He was portrayed in the major motion picture, *The Insider*, for his efforts in bringing down big tobacco. He had a saying that any lawyer could settle or work up a case. However, he wanted trial lawyers. Those capable of going into a courtroom and turning a case into gold.

The other category of lawyers are those that are about to take a case and polish it into a strong and favorable position. Those were mainly the students who did well in law school. They are able to analyze every case and issue to prepare the pending case in the best position to succeed.

Without the case in the door, the rest of it doesn't matter. You can have the brightest lawyers and the best trials. If they do not have cases to work on, your legal business will starve.

My law firm of Goldberg, Persky & White has always had all three of those types of lawyers. This is the reason we have excelled for decades in the asbestos world. I always prided myself on being capable of handling all three of those tasks. I now had the perfect case to show my talents and bring the case in, work it up, and beat the NFL in a trial. I did not blink twice when thinking about it. I believed that there was nothing to it. I simply wasn't intimidated by the NFL's team of lawyers from New York who were all tops of their Ivy League law schools. Or maybe I just felt that I could beat anyone on an even playing field. I figured that my law firm would throw a bunch of lawyers to assist me and we would take down this giant. We would be the most respected firm in the country with newfound money.

It turned out that getting this case started was not so simple yet again. I was ready to try out this case on my law firm. I figured that it would pique their interest. After all, it involved brain-damaged players and a huge cover-up by a ten-billion-dollar league.

I tried out the case on my younger associates and law clerks first. Like me, most of them were believers in the law and the facts. They believed it met the standards of a solid lawsuit that could be filed in court.

When I approached my friends, colleagues, and members of my firm with my idea to sue the NFL for brain injuries players developed from playing the game, I was met with the same skepticism and critiques that I still face in all football cases to this day. "These players knew the risk they were taking when they signed up to play the game" or that "the players true cause of death was not brain injury, but foolish risks taken after retirement." Those "foolish risks" to others remain the byproduct of brain injury suffered by former players. And while my legal team and I recognized this and believed in our mission to help former players suffering from brain damage that desperately needed our assistance, it was very difficult to convince those around me that my idea to go head to head against the biggest sports empire in the world for a risk inherent in playing the sport was a viable cause of action.

I was not giving up this easily. Bennet was my friend whose integrity and career was at stake. He needed help. I was determined to take this case to the highest ranks of my firm. I went and presented it to Pete Paladino. He was my supervisor and fell just below the named partners, Goldberg, Persky, and White, in rank at the firm. I recall stopping by his office and asking if I could talk with him about a new potential case.

Pete was always responsive to me. Maybe it was because he liked my thinking. It may have been because he saw me as a future leader in our business. He knew that his success as a leader was based in large part of the success of the younger lawyers. Pete was given opportunities to grow as a lawyer when times were very busy in the late '80s and early 1990s. He was running much like I did to depositions and trials. He appreciated his learning experience, and he saw in me that same motivation and did not want to dampen my desires as a lawyer. We were the type of lawyers who were hungry to impress. We would knock on doors and ask our superiors for more work. We would ask if there is anything to do. We would not sit back and do only what was in front of us.

When I went to Pete, as usual, I was welcomed and given the opportunity to talk to him. I recall going through all the details that I explained to the legal team. He did not say much during that first conversation. I recall his only thoughts were that the NFL was an 800-pound gorilla and that the players may not want to do this. I reassured him that they would be there for the fight. I left the meeting not knowing what he was thinking. I did not know if I would ever hear back from him on this issue.

I went back to business as an asbestos lawyer. I was working up more and more cases. At this point in time, another lawyer who had been given the opportunity to co-lead cases with me in my department had left the law firm. It was up to me to take the day-to-day lead in the department by myself. I too decided to give more opportunities to the younger lawyers. I started delegating assignments and giving them more chances to build their pedigree as lawyers. They were now doing more important tasks such as settling cases with defendants.

We were then asked by the courts in Allegheny County to move a backlogged docket of asbestos cases. There were a significant number of older filed cases that had been sitting in the court system and not moving quick enough. We were told and provided a scheduling order to move all these cases in clusters of fifty or more at a time. We were hiring more young lawyers and support staff. Things were busy enough to keep my mind off of the NFL.

However, my mind always drifted back to the case. I often wondered what I would do if my law firm decided not to go forward with the case. I couldn't just move on and forget about it. I owed it not only to Bennet, but I also owed it to the players.

Sometimes, I would go to the golf course and spend time with my friends. As usual, my golf friends always gave me a hard time for being a lawyer. However, the guys I golfed with really liked me. It probably had a lot to do with making myself and those who I meet feel at home. If you met me outside of work, you would never guess that I was a personal injury trial lawyer. Some of my golf friends happened to be doctors. Whenever I had the opportunity to tell people about the players' brain injuries and their personal struggles, I used it as a chance to test the merits of my claim.

One day, not too long after my conversation with Pete, I was back in the office. It seemed like I would only be in the office about two days per week. The rest of the time, I was on the road doing depositions or signing up new cases. I guess that is a lot better than the beginning of my career where I would spend five days a week on the road and weekends in the office. I was sitting at my desk when my phone rang. The caller identification noted that it was the fifth floor conference room.

I answered the phone and was asked by Ted Goldberg to come to the conference room. Walking down the hallway to the room, I could feel my nerves coursing up and down my body. When I opened the door to the conference room, I was greeted by one of the most intimidating sites a young lawyer can come upon: a dozen partners at the law firm sitting at the table.

I didn't get halfway into the room before the partners started asking me questions about the NFL case: "How do you know these players? Aren't their injuries related to steroids? Who is going to pay for this case?"

"In that moment, I stood there and paused as I digested the rapid-fire questions that came at me. Appreciating the difficult task I still had in convincing my firm to pursue this case, I took a deep breath and asked in a manner that gave the appearance of a calm and confident lawyer practicing well beyond his years "Would you mind if I found another firm to work with on this case?"

For what felt like hours in a room with a dozen skilled lawyers, they looked at each other blankly before one of the partners told me that I had their blessing to "Go find a sugar daddy" to fund my lawsuit against the NFL.

I left this meeting, which would have put most young lawyers down for the count, with a new sense of purpose and passion to pursue my case against the NFL and help these former players. When I got home, I shared this story with my wife Kelly who always believed in me. Sensing my passion and dedication to the cause, she told me point blank what the partners had told me earlier in the day: "go find another law firm to fight this battle." With that, I was off to the races to talk to anyone and everyone who would give me the time and support to go after the NFL.

CHAPTER 16

Finding a Friend in Jack

After my conversation with the partners and with Kelly, I returned to the office the next day and bumped into an individual who would become integral to my continued efforts to sue the NFL, Jack Tierney. Jack had heard about what happened at the partners meeting the previous day and couldn't wait to offer his assistance in my mission to help former NFL players.

Jack Tierney wasn't your normal lawyer. He was a beast with a kind heart. Jack graduated from Stanford University with an undergraduate degree. Then he went on to graduate Georgetown University law school. He finished near the top in his graduating classes. After clerking for a federal judge, Jack spent the early part of his career working as a defense lawyer in railroad litigation cases. He worked at the Pittsburgh powerhouse insurance and corporate defense firm of Reed Smith. The Reed Smith law firm housed hundreds, if not thousands, of lawyers working by the minute for countless hours each day. Jack spent his time there learning how to defend railroads against lawsuits. He learned the art of creating papers, motions, briefs, and then defending them, often successfully, at trial.

Jack was a detail-oriented lawyer that would spend endless hours on files. He saw that as his means to win the case. The more time you spent knowing the issue inside and out, the more likely that you will win.

Over the course of his career at Reed Smith, Jack ultimately burnt out from working. Some people rumored that he even had a nervous breakdown. Ultimately, he was picked up as a lawyer by my firm in the 1990s. He was typically given an individual case or two to solve. Most of the time, those cases involved ERISA matters where a person or group of employees were cheated out of a pension benefit that was owed to them by law.

Jack and I first met when I was a law clerk at Goldberg Persky & White in the late 1990s. Jack always seemed to have a way of locating the new law clerks to help him with a trivial issue on a research project. Sometimes, he liked the law clerks helping to answer written discovery requests. I think he preferred using us as opposed to secretaries or paralegals, as the number of times he would make edits would drive the staff completely crazy. Law clerks, on the other hand, were young and eager to please.

I was your typical law clerk. I was always eager to help Jack. After all, it was yet another lawyer I could try to impress. Assuming that it never interfered with my regular duties, Jack knew that he could rely on me as his personal law clerk at times.

When I became a full-time employee in 2000, Jack had a case against a major corporation in Pittsburgh that committed age discrimination in firing all of their salaried employees over the age of fifty. Jack was able to uncover smoking guns from the company's CEO stating that the company needed to get rid of the "deadwood."

Jack was a good lawyer to have on your side. He gave you an advantage in your practice by having a lawyer with so much and so vast of a past legal career spanning many decades.

More than anything, Jack is one of those rare people you meet in life that truly loved his job. He was married to it fully and unconditionally. There was nothing more that he looked forward to than working on legal matters. In fact, he had little to no hobbies outside of work. Years later, when I asked him what he would like to do on his retirement, he said that he wanted to practice law.

Jack was eager to get involved with the NFL case. Like the perfect teammate, the first question he asked me was what he could do to help me. I immediately wanted him to get him involved researching the prior cases where the NFL was sued and lost. I also wanted to see if he could find anything in the collective bargaining agreements where the NFL discussed this concussion problem. I wanted an experienced lawyer to actually double check what I had already done. I wanted to make sure that my legal analysis was correct.

Away he went. Jack was completely engulfed in papers. As usual, it was disorganized chaos that only he could relate to. There was case after case reprinted. There would be eight copies of the same two-hundred-page CBA reprinted. Other cases involving similar issues and many copies would be sprawled all over his desk.

Jack was known to be persistent in his methodology. When he needed something, he would continue to pick up the phone and call the person. Sometimes, he would leave a dozen messages in one day just because he needed something that he could not put his fingers on, and it would be the obstacle that he needed to overcome before he could move on to the next phase. His persistence often annoyed many people he came in contact with.

On occasion, his persistence would drive me crazy. He would continue to ring my office phone, and if I did not answer, he would call my cellphone. If that did not work, it was the paging system in the office. If still unsuccessful in locating me, he would call my assistant. By that time, she would start calling my phone to tell me that Jack wanted to speak with me. Most often, the call was not even important. Sometimes, Jack loved the law so much that he would just call to quote me language from a judge's opinion that I had already read a number of times in the past during my investigation of this case.

As much as he would frustrate me, he was a welcome addition. My first lawyer to truly commit to the case. I felt that our team could only grow from here.

CHAPTER 17

Shopping the Case

Many personal injury law firms across the country handle asbestos cases. We often work together and share resources and knowledge. I always offered to help others. In turn, other firms would help me when I asked. I struggled to think of a good fit for the NFL case. I could not think of anyone in my rolodex that would be the right fit for this case.

Over the years, I had become close friends with John Comerford. John is a lawyer from Buffalo, New York, who handles asbestos cases as well. John and I had become close for a number of reasons, including sharing clients and materials as well as both being from blue-collar Catholic families. John and I also had a mutual friend in Aaron DeLuca. Aaron was one of my mentors who had left my law firm in late 2003. We always called to laugh about our stories of Aaron, who sadly died unexpectedly in 2011.

I called John Comerford on the phone one day and tried out my case on him. I told him what my law firm had said about the case. He did not say much. I asked him who would be a good fit for this case. He did not have a response.

I asked John if he had any thoughts about what I should do. He gave me one of those "let me think about it" type of answers. Years later, he admitted to me that he did not see a legal case on behalf of the former players, and he did not want me to hurt my credibility and confidence shopping the case.

I must not have read his signals well. I assumed I hit him with a huge legal matter that he was not prepared to discuss with me.

John and I did agree that this case needed a powerful trial lawyer, someone who was willing to invest their time and money in this case. It needed a lawyer who could take on a very public battle with confidence and with competence.

We started talking about big time lawyers and who was connected with these types of lawyers. I ultimately asked him about Mark Lanier. This was the Houston lawyer that my mentor Aaron Deluca went to work for in late 2003. Aaron had since moved on to open his own private practice.

I asked him about what he knew about Mark Lanier and if Aaron had any bad experiences. He said that Mark was an outstanding trial lawyer. He had recently won a $250,000,000 verdict in the first Vioxx drug case that received a favorable verdict. Aaron just had aspirations of running his own business, and that was the main reason he left Mark Lanier's law firm. John continued that Mark Lanier was highly charismatic and would relish the spotlight of a case of this magnitude.

Mark Lanier had grown his firm from a two-person practice in Texas to over a sixty-lawyer law firm that had offices in California, New York, and Texas. Mark obtained a 118-million-dollar verdict in an asbestos case. Recently, he received a $56,000,000 verdict in a case involving a crippled man from a machinery company. Mark was one of the most successful lawyers in the country and was recognized in every legal publication for his achievements. He also spent a considerable amount of time preaching and teaching at a Baptist Christian Church in Houston, Texas.

I thanked John for being such a good friend and always being so helpful. He cautioned me that it could be difficult and wished me well. I knew he meant it. John, years later, showed his true friendship when he announced my success to the entire plaintiff trial lawyer community that I was the lawyer to congratulate for this case.

I knew that I needed to get this case in front of Mark Lanier. I did not know him personally. Certainly, he did not know me. I doubt he would just take my cold telephone call. I needed someone on the inside to pitch it to Mark. But who and how?

In recent years, I made a connection at the Lanier firm from referring a couple of asbestos victims to them to handle the case since the guys worked in Texas. Like almost every big law firm that specialized in representing injured parties, they all had an asbestos department, and Mark Lanier's firm was no different.

My contact was with a young lawyer, Angela. I wanted to make a rehearsed phone call with a marketing pitch to the young lawyer who brought Mark Lanier his next big case. I needed her to first buy into the case.

I made the call and told her that I had the smoking gun as to the NFL's cover-up of concussions. There are many former players dying at young ages from football's version of punch-drunk syndrome. I could get these cases to Mark, and I am close friends with the doctor who uncovered it all. I left the short call with a next step message that we could put a meeting together with Mark to discuss.

I thought the call went well. She said the she would be back with me. I figured that I would send a follow-up e-mail in a day or two reminding her of this conversation and telling her some additional specific facts in the e-mail message to pique her interest.

I did not need to send it. By the end of the day, she sent me an e-mail that their firm was extremely interested. She explained that someone else would be my contact form this point forward. She thanked me for reaching out to her. Certainly, I hoped that by doing so I helped her career in the law firm.

Over the next few days, I wondered who I would hear from at Lanier's firm. Ultimately, I received a message from Evan Janush from Mark's New York City office. They wanted to schedule a meeting with them in their office. They would be happy to fly me up at their cost.

We found an agreeable date in the next week or so, and off I went to prepare for the big meeting. I was going to over-prepare myself for the meeting. I would have every issue typed up with citations to the appropriate sources. I was prepared to leave my notes with them.

I arrived at the Lanier law firm in midtown Manhattan. It was spotless and picturesque. I sat in the waiting area and saw the articles in magazines naming Mark one of the top lawyers in the country. I was a little nervous and anxious waiting. All trial lawyers feel that way. However, we know how to channel those feelings into confidence and charisma. For me, it took a lot of preparation of my material, practice, knowledge of the issue, and familiarity with arguing in front of judges. The last, and my personal secret, was always respecting the fact that my client sought out a lawyer for help in a time of need. They needed a champion at their moment of most need due to their failing health. I would picture myself as the best lawyer like one of those famous lawyers from the movies. I would study them and work on portraying their confidence and charisma and be polite and positive despite my opponent's experience, age, or distinguished career.

I walked into the conference room and was introduced to two lawyers, Rick Meadow and Evan Janush. These guys quickly alerted me that Mark could not make the meeting due to a scheduling change. This news instantly took the wind out of my sails. However, they quickly responded that Mark goes for any new cases that they pitch to him. After all, he entrusted the two of them to run an office he owned in the business and financial mecca of the world. It made me instantly feel at ease with the two of them.

Rick Meadow was a polished lawyer that had vast knowledge of tort cases. He spent a considerable amount of his practice handling and administrating the mass tort practice at Mark's firm. He had served on chairs of committees overseeing nationwide pharmaceutical cases. He was well aware of the important issues that made a case viable and good versus a waste of resources.

I ultimately ended up spending more time with Evan Janush. Evan was an incredibly intelligent lawyer. He was young, personable, energetic, and also showed charisma. He did not look like one of those legal brainiacs. Rather, he looked like a guy who belonged in a courtroom. His background was impressive. He graduated from the Benjamin Cardozo School of Law in New York, where he was on law review and was president of the Student Bar Association. Evan's career involved supporting many appeals, motions, and oral arguments that supported trial verdicts of Mark Lanier. Evan was a sponge to Mark and the other lawyers; not only did he watch them closely, he soaked in their leadership and skills and polished it into a perfected product that he utilized as his own style.

I sat across from them in a fancy conference room to discuss the brain damage lawsuit against the NFL. I remember them asking me to explain who these scientists and doctors were and why I believed there was a legal claim. I was no more than about ten minutes into my presentation when it struck me how attentive they were to what I was saying and how polite and respectful they were to me. They made me feel like the expert. In turn, I was impressed with these two lawyers. I had never seen lawyers so knowledgeable about legal issues. They were in tune with science. They understood brain injury. It was as if they were playing this case out loud in the trial as I was explaining it. I wondered if these lawyers were an anomaly.

The meeting finished after lunch in the conference room. They rented a limousine to take me to LaGuardia Airport. It was a beautiful spring day in New York City. The sun was shining. The weather was warm enough to take off my suit coat. I felt good. I felt that once Evan and Rick pitched this case to Mark Lanier, then we would be battling in court with the NFL on behalf of Dr. Omalu and the former players.

CHAPTER 18

Preparing the Complaint

It was not long before I heard back from Evan Janush who told me that Mark Lanier was interested. It was evident that Evan was going to be my person of contact on this case. It also became very clear that Evan was going to have to become Mark's expert on this case. He would need to digest everything there is to know and then be able to defend it as the player's advocate.

Evan explained that Mark needed to see a complaint. A complaint is the legal instrument that sets forth the legal and factual reasons for a civil lawsuit brought against a wrongdoer that is filed to start the court action. I was not surprised that Mark wanted to see a complaint. I was, however, shocked that they wanted me to draft it in large part.

I must have really had them fooled. Here I was, Jason Luckasevic, graduating in the bottom three of his law school class of Duquesne University, drafting a complaint that would be defended by the best, the brightest, and most highly paid Ivy League distinguished career lawyers. I giggled and told Evan that I would get working on it immediately.

In the practice of law, there is no copyright protection. I knew that I could use the language right out of past complaints that were filed of public record. I went and did just that and searched the dockets of Brown, Williams, and Stringer to locate the language that was successfully used in those cases.

I also asked Jack Tierney for some federal complaints that he did in the past. I was curious with style, grammar and, most importantly, making sure it said what it need to legally so that it would not be thrown out of court on a technicality.

I often took my materials home to work on at night. I would spend weekends drafting the complaint. I took this job very seriously. This was the ultimate paperwork that would vindicate my friend, Dr. Bennet Omalu.

When starting out with a complaint, the most important first steps are to make sure that you have correctly identified the companies you are suing. You also need to make sure that you have named all of them, even their subsidiaries where applicable.

I knew that my complaint needed to follow *Stringer*. There was no case ever against the NFL that I could correlate as closer to this brain damage crisis than the *Stringer* case. Like *Stringer*, I was convinced that we needed to sue not only the NFL but also NFL Properties and Riddell, the helmet maker.

Helmets were used as a weapon by many football players. The law requires manufacturers to maintain an adequate warning on any product. If you sell headache medicine, you must place a label on your bottle that states that too much dosage can cause you to overdose. Riddell did not adequately warn about brain damage. In fact, it was not until recent years that they started to place a warning sticker on their helmets that contained some vague language that a helmet does not protect from a concussion. On top of that, they could not argue that there is labor preemption much like the NFL would. Rather, the Stringers successfully showed Riddell's responsibility and ultimate failure to sell safe equipment in the court case.

If I was using *Stringer* as the model, it was apparent that both the NFL and NFL Properties needed to be sued. The *Stringer* Court found that there was no preemption as to the legal claim that NFL and NFL Properties failed in their duty to license safe equipment.

After I determined who to sue, we needed to confirm where they were located and incorporated. It sounded easy, but it turned out to be complicated. For instance, the NFL was an unincorporated association with tax exempt status. They were headquartered in New

York. However, for purposes of determining what or what states they practiced and did business in was quite confusing. Were they citizens of every state there is a team? What about Hawaii, where they held the Pro Bowl? Figuring this out was very important to the ultimate determination of what court had jurisdiction. In other words, we had to locate the proper state to determine where we could file the lawsuit. If we didn't do that, our lawsuit could be dismissed as soon as it is filed for failing to properly file it in a court and state that was permitted to hear the dispute.

Riddell, the helmet manufacturing company, was even more complex. They had created holding companies, different divisions, and related corporations. If we did not find a proper state and forum in which to file, we would run the risk of having our case transferred to another court. If we did not find the proper place, we could be transferred to a state where none of us were licensed to practice.

Making these mistakes are critical, embarrassing, and penal, much like committing a false start penalty in a football game.

After I figured out these matters, it was off to putting forth all the facts that set forth the basis of the lawsuit. I traced the origins of the MTBI Committee, the findings of Dr. Omalu, the attack by the NFL doctors on him when he attempted to publish his findings, and then the NFL's efforts to produce contrary scientific and medical findings regarding head injuries in the NFL.

I covered the stories of Mike Webster, Terry Long, Andre Waters, and Justin Strzelczyk. I included information about players forced to retire due to post-concussion syndrome. It included all of the rule changes in the NFL involving head contact over the last four decades. It talked about the ban of the head slap by the defensive player on the offensive lineman. It talked about the personal file penalty for face masking. The complaint talked about the banning of the helmet to helmet hits. It additionally included the medical articles I located concerning the ill effects of repeated and cumulative concussions and sub-concussions. Finally, it included some of the early media coverage on the NFL's actions regarding concussions.

Once the parties and facts giving rise to the lawsuit were established, I needed to raise the legal claims. Civil lawsuits generally consist of claims of negligence and strict liability claims for failure to properly warn of known dangers. For this, I looked at the Stringer and Brown Complaints and court opinions on this issue. I wanted our legal claims to be air tight so that the NFL could not distinguish the court's findings and opinions wherein they found no labor preemption.

The most difficult task of doing this was setting forth what duty the NFL has and how they failed to act upon it. It was clear the NFL assumed the duty to study and report on head injuries when they created the MTBI Committee. However, it was a longstanding duty that went as far back as their collective bargaining agreements wherein they included player safety provisions and when they adopted rules and often changed them to protect the players.

What should they have done differently? If you hold a duty of care and someone is injured because of your failure, what exactly was that failure? I explained that the NFL needed to alert the players that repeated head traumas cause latent later-life problems. They should have properly identified the injured players and provided them with adequate injury prevention and recovery techniques. There needed to be return to play guidelines and protocol from independent physicians that did not have a stake in the outcomes of the games.

The draft of the complaint also included a legal claim against the NFL and NFL Properties for failing to license safe helmets. Then, finally, it included claims against Riddell for failing to license a helmet with a proper warning concerning the long term risks of repeated head trauma.

I felt positive I had created the backdrop of the NFL concussion lawsuit by April 2007. I figured all that was left to do was to get some edits from smart lawyers like Evan, and then Mark Lanier would file it. All I had to do in the meantime would be to figure out what former players needed to be plaintiffs.

CHAPTER 19

Cold Feet

As life would have it, I was learning a cruel lesson on how difficult the practice of law was. I was beginning to truly respect my profession and appreciate the stories of how difficult life is as a lawyer. This process of ups and downs made me very appreciative of the time invested in cases without any certainty of recovery.

Then, like a continuous cruel joke, I received more disappointing news. Mark Lanier was not ready to file. He wanted more information. He wanted to see the past collective bargaining agreements and the current players' contracts. He had a hard time believing that the NFL and their lawyers would not put waiver language somewhere concerning head injuries. Evan called to also tell me that Mark wanted to know what smoking gun documents existed. I thought to myself, smoking gun documents? Umm…well…what's wrong with their unscientific publications in the medical journals, I wanted to respond. Evan asked how we determine these answers. I knew of the perfect person. We needed to ask Chris Nowinski.

Chris was the Harvard-educated former WWE wrestler who was quickly becoming the authority on head injuries in the NFL due to his book and his newly formed non-profit with Dr. Omalu and Dr. Bailes and Dr. Cantu seeking out brains to perform autopsies. I told Evan that we needed to meet with Chris and ask him if he could provide anything further that I did not already possess.

I reached out to Chris immediately. He was always so quick to respond. I told him about my efforts and my teaming up with the Lanier law firm. I told him that Evan and I would like to have a phone call to explore our questions. The call was set up in a few days. We had a conference call, and soon thereafter, we had a face-to-face meeting in Boston. Chris believed he could help us with these documents. We figured Chris had these types of documents at his fingertips, or he could find them rather quickly. Further, our efforts to bring a lawsuit could only help raise awareness to their group about players donating their brains to them.

Evan and I were agreeable to paying Nowinski a retainer of $5,000 for his time. We figured we would not need that much work out of him. The alternative was for us to spend countless hours trying to track down these documents. We would monitor his hours so as not to cost us too much money.

In less than a week, Chris gave us collective bargaining agreements, player contracts, and some miscellaneous other documents. It satisfied Mark Lanier's curiosity about the waiver issue. There was nothing in the player's contracts stating that they assumed the risk of a long-term chronic brain injury problem at the time they signed their player contracts. It just did not exist. On the other hand, as expected, there were no other smoking guns that I had not already discovered.

There was nothing that could stop the NFL from facing a lawsuit by us for their improper handling of the former player's brain injuries. Once again, I was wrong yet again. When I went back to the players I had met, they instantly got cold feet. The gravity of the situation frightened them. They would sue the sport that made them who they are for not protecting their brains. What kind of a man were they? They just could not bring themselves to joining at this point. It hit me like a ton of bricks. Maybe I was a fool for doing all this work. I am sure all of those who were critical would be laughing at me shortly.

I was so close to making this case a reality. I could not give up due to this setback. There were over 15,000 former NFL players. It was inevitable that some of them would want to pursue this case.

I told Evan that we should ask Chris to introduce us to more folks. Chris Nowinski soon introduced us to a couple of new people. One of the players had an athletic agent involved. Ultimately, the agent started calling Evan behind my back and was pushing to cut himself into the case. The agent did not think I needed to be involved as Mark Lanier was big enough to do this case without me. Evan quickly told me of this experience. Evan not only set the guy straight that this case would not exist without my efforts, but he also told this sports agent that he was not getting cut into the case. Then he told me that there was never any question with their law firm about my name attached directly with this lawsuit and the complaint. This was the first time an attempt was made to toss me to the side on my efforts to make this case happen. It also would prove later on to not be the last time this would happen.

I was glad Evan stuck up for me. It felt good to see that someone had my back. We ultimately quietly distanced ourselves from this player and his agent.

Not to worry, Chris said he had a friend that would be the perfect candidate. This former player won multiple Super Bowls. He was younger. He also had a documented history of being mistreated while suffering a concussion that was documented in media publishings. He was struggling physically, mentally, and functionally. He would spend days without leaving his house. He would remain in a dark room for days. His head constantly pounded. He simply could not function. This lasted years after he left the game.

The four of us all met together in Boston. The meeting went well. The former player seemed to really feel at ease with me. In turn, he was impressed with Lanier's firm as Evan relayed it to him. We left him with a retainer agreement and figured that he was all in to take on the NFL.

After a week of not hearing back from the former player, we asked Chris if he has heard from his friend. Chris said he would look into it and get back to us. We were not satisfied with Chris's influence over the former player. Therefore, Evan and I had to find out where this player stood. We ultimately received an e-mail from the former player thanking us for our efforts and wishing us luck. He did not wish to sue the NFL as it would create a conflict of interest for him as he still had hopes of coaching in the National Football

League. Down the road, he never became a coach, but he did join the lawsuit many years later.

This point reached a new low for me. It even brought Evan down. We had so much hope to pull this together. Now, the players do not want to help themselves. I thought to myself that this case may after all prove to be impossible.

CHAPTER 20

Key Additions

If I thought this case was impossible in May, two months later, I almost started believing that it was hopeless. Right after the fireworks ended on the Fourth of July, Kelly went into labor. The next day, our miracle daughter, Addison, was born. We struggled for years hoping to someday have a baby, but it just did not happen. All of our friends had kids, but we were not blessed. Then all of the sudden, we were blessed to find out that Kelly was pregnant with Addison. My mom, who always wanted a girl, was the happiest person in the world.

We brought Addison home to her crib positioned under Tinkerbell and her famous quote, "All you need is faith, trust, and a little pixie dust." This brought instant changes to everything. Kelly was now working part-time from home writing legal decisions for federal judges. I was going to have to be the breadwinner for our new family. Addison also created new priorities and more structure for us.

I was also busy with my asbestos case load. The year 2007 may have been our busiest year ever as a law firm. At least our Western Pennsylvania caseload was larger than ever. I was also fortunate to have my assistant, Cindy DeUnger. I hired Cindy in 2004. She came from a background with paralegal and secretarial experience at some large successful plaintiff firms where she worked on big tobacco cases.

She recently moved back home to the Pittsburgh area after her husband, who served twenty-five years in the navy, retired. As much as Jack Tierney was committed to me, Cindy proved to be even more committed. On top of that, she became my close friend, and we consider her, her husband (Joe), and their daughter (Beth), part of our family.

Cindy is the best of workers. She does everything. She does it correctly, and regularly works extra hours. Her work ethic and efforts to help clients has been immensely beneficial and all of the clients love her.

I went into 2008 with the mindset that I would have my best year ever career wise. I also found out that baby number two was due in the summer. My hope was also to pull this NFL case together. I was monitoring the league closely in the news and media. I watched games to see if there were any changes as to how concussed players were being cared for by the trainers and medical staff.

Just shortly into the new year, Bennet sent me an e-mail stating that his group, The Sports Legacy Institute non-profit, split up. Dr. Omalu, Dr. Bailes, Atty. Bob Fitzsimmons, and Mike Webster's son, Garrett, formed BIRI (Brain Injury Research Institute) in West Virginia. Chris Nowinski and Dr. Cantu left to join their non-profit with Boston University.

For much of 2008, Bennet was entrenched with a personal struggle. He was now dealing with people in his inner circle that he mistrusted in business dealings. Bennet withdrew away, much like myself, from this NFL piece during most of the year. We believed we were helping those in need. We were disheartened to see that others did not view things the same.

My second daughter, Alexis, was born on June 30. She came into the world with the biggest smile and blue eyes brighter than mine. She quickly came to fall in love with her Irish twin sister, Addison, and figured out that our dog, Nala, was her personal play toy. And, of course, Kelly and my mom were thrilled to have two girls. This made her and my dad and my grandmother come to our house almost daily.

CHAPTER 21

Omalu and My Friendship during Tough Times

With our second child, it got to the point where we had to make a decision about child care issues with our family. We needed to decide whether Kelly should get another job, or continue her job, or become a full-time mom. After weighing all the pros and cons, we decided that Kelly should move on to the most important career of all. She became a full-time stay at home mom to Addison and Alexis.

Therefore, I had to be disciplined at work. Our young family was completely relying on me financially. Kelly, by nature, was not a risk taker. Therefore, she did not want to hear about the concussion case. I decided to keep my focus on work. I would not talk about any news on the concussion case at home. It was not that difficult of a task since there was not much going on in 2008.

Bennet's life changed dramatically around this time as well. It all started when his boss, the renowned Dr. Cyril Wecht, came under federal investigation. He ultimately was indicted on a number of charges involving using his public office, the Allegheny County Medical Examiner's Office, for private work. Prosecutors charged Dr. Wecht with using a taxpayer position to make money personally. The prosecution went after Dr. Omalu much like the NFL. They wanted Dr. Omalu to be the key witness to testify against his mentor and boss. If he did not, he would face the ultimate penalty of being told to leave the country.

Dr. Wecht was forced to step down from his position as chief medical examiner. Dr. Omalu, in turn, left to move 2,000 miles away to San Joaquin County, California, and accept a position of chief medical examiner. As irony would have it, a new medical examiner was appointed by the name of Dr. Karl Williams. One of his first hires was none other than my brother, Dr. Todd Luckasevic, as assistant medical examiner in Allegheny County.

My brother moved back home to the Pittsburgh region within ten minutes of my house. After spending the last few years in Virginia and Washington DC, our family was really happy to be back together again.

As Dr. Wecht's criminal case proceeded to trial, Dr. Omalu was very upset. We would stay in touch by speaking early in the mornings. He usually called around 7:30 in the morning, which would be 4:30 a.m. in California. The conversations were typically depressing. He seemed to be no longer testing brains of players who were dying. He often inquired if I was having any success pulling the lawsuit together. Even though I felt that the case was hopeless, I gave him hope that I would pull this together. He deserved it. In my opinion, he deserved the highest recognition for his discovery of CTE, maybe even the Nobel Prize.

Ultimately, Dr. Omalu had to go to trial and testify against Dr. Wecht. It was a highly publicized case where every county employees were brought into trial to explain what was going at the Allegheny County Medical Examiner's Office. Dr. Omalu was called to the stand to explain how he was asked to do private matters for Dr. Wecht during work hours while in office.

Bennet went to trial and testified. He had no choice. He was rather diplomatic with the questions being asked by the prosecutor. He came into town quickly and left even quicker to return home to California.

By the end of the trial, the prosecution was unable to convince the jury that Dr. Wecht was guilty criminally for using his public funded office as a private business.

During this period of time, I would continually be asked about the status of the NFL concussion case. This was incredibly difficult on me emotionally. For the first time in my life, I felt like a failure. It was a horrible feeling to not pull off something despite putting my best efforts into making it happen. I thought that maybe I was just not good enough.

Bennet and I were depressed. We felt completely alone. During this time, the only thing that held us together was our commitment to each other. He trusted me with this lawsuit. He could have taken it to any lawyer in the United States, but he trusted me. I, likewise, believed in Bennet's findings of CTE in the former players when no one else did. I was committed to protecting his integrity. Even during these difficult times, we believed in each other that we would hold up to our end of the bargain.

CHAPTER 22

Eyes on the League and Speaking at Conferences

I was keeping a close eye on the NFL going into 2009. I figured that it would not be long before they would make some major mistakes with concussions that could influence former players to file the lawsuit with me. I went to the AFC Championship game. Then it was on to the Super Bowl in Tampa, Florida.

I traveled with two of my close golf buddies, Joel Sherman and Daryl King. The Pittsburgh Steelers were back in the Super Bowl, and the following of the team could not have been bigger in their pursuit of an NFL record sixth Super Bowl.

We traveled for a memorable experience to Tampa, Florida. We even managed to crash Leigh Steinberg's party and saw many interesting celebrities and former athletes along the way, including Dennis Rodman. Our seats were on the fifteen-yard line about a dozen rows from the field. We watched one of the greatest Super Bowls of all time. I will always remember the interception by James Harrison at the goal line right before halftime and him running toward our corner of the end zone and scoring. I was present for the play that will go down as one of the greatest in Super Bowl history.

James Harrison would soon become the poster child for the concussion issue. He was fined $120,000 in total fines for several hits, penalties, and fouls which the NFL deemed to be illegal. It was the first time ever that the NFL disciplined anyone for issues relating to concussions.

Placing blame on the players became the platform that the NFL wanted to endorse as their next defensive strategy. James Harrison was their perfect villain to showcase that the players were personally at fault for the concussion problems. In the meantime, the NFL was, behind the scenes, selling images of James Harrison's knockout hits for a profit. This was further proof that the NFL marketed violence and head injury.

As another example of their despicable behavior, the NFL passed out a concussion brochure to all current players. Not surprisingly, they failed to send anything to the retired players. Regardless, the information distributed to the active players was from their own flawed findings. The pamphlet stated, "There is no magic number of how many concussions is too many." Once again, the NFL's stance on concussions and CTE was a spit in the face of Dr. Omalu. Additionally, it was a hoax to anyone who played the game of football and modeled their rules and league after the NFL.

The concussion pamphlet also provided the NFL further cover to their responsibility. The pamphlet instructed players to report their own concussion symptoms. It stated that if you have concussion symptoms, you (the player) should immediately report your symptoms to team doctors and trainers. Once again, they required the brain injured player to be responsible for his injury.

The NFL also delegated responsibility on the team to obtain independent doctors to return players to play after sustaining a concussion. This was laughable that they believed a player could return after concussion, possibly even to the same game.

The retired players were closely watching this developing saga. Despite the fact that the league continued to ignore them in their communications, the retired players were paying attention and reading the news reports. They were starting to band together and discuss their similar problems on internet blog sites. It was alarming that so many of them were having problems beyond the expected orthopedic issues.

In 2009, a number of retired players held a summit in Las Vegas to meet and discuss a plan. They put together a seminar that included various lawyers speaking on NFL disability, worker's compensation, and publicity rights. They had other presenters planned to discuss brain donation and various issues surrounding Plan 88. Plan 88 was a disability plan named after John Mackey, who was a Hall-of-Fame tight end for the Baltimore Colts. John Mackey at one point became the union president for the players association. In recent times, John Mackey was diagnosed with dementia. His wife, Sylvia, advocated to the NFL to create a medical benefit for players with dementia, Parkinson's, and Alzheimer's. Ultimately, the NFL created a benefit due to the higher rates for former players coming down with these neurological conditions. However, the applications for Plan 88 specifically denied any link to these conditions being caused by football. Therefore, upon approval of his application, the player qualified for reimbursement of costs up to $88,000 in medical care.

I saw this summit as a perfect opportunity to present my idea of a brain injury lawsuit to a large number of former players. I instantly called the former players running the conference and asked if I could have ten minutes to present on a lawsuit that I was going to file against the NFL. I pushed and pushed the organizers until I received my invite to the summit and opportunity to speak.

I arrived at the two-day conference, which was free to all former players. It was held at the Southpointe Casino located off of the Las Vegas Strip. The rooms were provided to the players at reduced rates of under seventy-five dollars per night. They also offered the former players free or reduced prices on their meals. I expected to walk into a room of thousands of former players. I was stunned that there were less than 100 people in a huge ballroom conference center.

Like we have become accustomed to watching on Sundays, the conference started with a prayer and the singing of the national anthem. The organizers then asked everyone to introduce themselves. I took notes as quickly as possible. In all, there were about eighty-five people. Less than fifty were former NFL players. There were about another dozen who were wives of the players. There were even a handful of newly appointed officers with the NFL Players Association.

The stories took me back in time over two years ago when I was interviewing former players and their spouses. The only difference was that time made their brain injuries progress. Yet with the passing of two years, there still was no help by the NFL for its former players.

I was given fifteen minutes to present after a group of lawyers finished talking about a publicity rights lawsuit against the NFL. I took my PowerPoint and went through fifteen minutes of the NFL's lies to the players and how a lawsuit could be based on the Korey Stringer and Orlando Brown cases. They all paid close attention, especially the officers from the players' association. When it was over, they allowed time for questions. Most of the people were former players and spouses discussing their problems and thanking me for trying to help them. Then I was questioned by a workers' compensation lawyer.

For years, many players only hope of getting anything from the league they served was filing a worker's compensation lawsuit. Under California law, if a player played at least one career game in California, he could file a lawsuit for his injuries. The best thing about the law was that it allowed you to file decades after you retired from the game. The market was led by a few former players who became lawyers after they retired from football. Those lawyers treated it like an assembly line by sending the players to the same doctors and ultimately settling their claims between $50,000 and $150,000 based on the severity of their injuries. In crafting the deals, they made sure they put 20 percent in their pockets while generally releasing all claims dealing with brain injuries. They also routinely dismissed their right to a lifetime of medical care provided by the insurance carriers.

Around 2011, these lawyers started adding claims to include their brain injuries to the settlement amidst pressure from the former players. Regardless of this effort, I even had a call recently from a client's wife asking me my opinion about what I thought of a settlement offer made by a team her husband had played twelve years for in the 1970s. This player was diagnosed with dementia fourteen years ago. He was constantly seeing neuro-specialists and undergoing a significant battery of tests. He qualified for the Plan 88 disability benefit ten years ago. He had regular home nursing care. To say the least, any life had vanished many years ago. His workers' compensation lawyer called him both excited and pushy to offer him and his wife what he dubbed a fair settlement of $75,000. It was these types of lawyers and situations that caused these players to be so skeptical of the league, lawyers, or anyone who believed they were trying to help them.

One of the worker's compensation lawyers was a former Los Angeles Ram. When I had finished my discussion about the concussion case at the Las Vegas Summit, he quickly used this opportunity to tell the players there was no legal basis to bring a lawsuit against the NFL as their only right to recovery was through a worker's compensation system that was working just fine for him. I quickly defended the case just as I did in the past. I quickly bit back that brain injuries are worth more than $100,000 and that past cases have been successful against the NFL. I could not believe this lawyer, and more importantly, he was a former player who was so adverse to the massive brain injury lawsuit. Years later, this lawyer advised players who he represented that they should file these cases. To show the true colors of some people close to the NFL, he later filed a class action against the NHL alleging the same problems despite the NHL being light years ahead of the NFL and actually creating concussion protocol.

I know that my presentation would leave them wanting to join. I told them just enough to make them contact me and the comment about not only looking for $100,000 would get them all talking about me and my case.

During the next break, players walked up to me and asked me for my business card. I gave multiple cards to every player with my cellphone number as well. I made sure I got contact information for each of them. Then I went through the same process over and over again with the same former players. They had no recollection that we had just spoken.

I grabbed the red-eye back that Saturday evening and went over my notes during the four-hour flight. I was way too excited to sleep. I could not wait to tell Bennet of my new hope to file.

CHAPTER 23

Time to Find Another
Co-Counsel

Bennet was excited to hear the news. He told me that he never doubted me that I would pull this together. I needed to send Evan at Lanier's office a message updating him of the summit. I was certain he would be thrilled.

After not hearing a response from Evan, I tried calling him and left another message. I didn't get a response from these as well. I could not believe it. I tried more e-mails and calls over the next couple of weeks with continued silence. I was completely confused. Had Evan left the firm? I checked their website, and he was still on their roster. Maybe he was in trial. I would give it another week. I did not want to get to the point of being obnoxious. I, however, was quite concerned about his lack of response and whether they were still interested in the case.

About another week passed, and I finally received an e-mail from Evan expressing that the Lanier firm was no longer interested in pursuing the case against the NFL. The e-mail didn't say more than circumstances had changed in their opinion. I was dumbfounded. What circumstances have changed? I chalked it up to another obstacle in the unending road to bring this case to a courtroom. I did not want to pester Evan. I was disappointed as I really liked my working relationship with them. I could not dwell on their decision. I had to move on from that law firm.

That left me back to where it all started. A growing case and no one interested to take on the eight-hundred-pound gorilla besides me and my friend, Bennet, armed with the loose change in our pockets and our ambitious young naïve minds.

At this time, I had a growing list of inquiries of players interested in filing a lawsuit. I, however, was now back to square one with no lawyers to lead the case. I figured that I had once again regressed three years in time on this case. I was hard pressed on what to do next. I figured this case would eventually be chalked up as a waste of my time if no other lawyers in the country had my initiative and eagerness to fight injustice and take on this multibillion dollar league.

The list of interested players continued to grow after I spoke at another retired player conference in Las Vegas the next year. There was not much difference in the conference in the spring of 2010 from the prior year. The turnout was horrifically low. In fact, I somehow think that the turnout in 2010 was even worse. Players just did not have a couple hundred dollars to pay for a few days in Las Vegas. It's hard to even imagine that former NFL professional football players didn't have enough extra money to pay for a few days in Vegas.

By then, my phone number and e-mail address was making its circles in the retired player community. I was being talked about by my heroes. They were discussing that I was someone willing to fight for their needs. I would get a few calls and e-mails from players every week wishing me well and telling me that they supported what I was trying to do.

Soon after the conference, I happened to bump into one of my partners in our downtown Pittsburgh office. Bruce Mattock was a nice guy that always was kind and friendly to every employee, including me. He seemed to have a knack for talking up our law firm's results and getting new business in the door. He asked me how things were coming along with the NFL case I was trying to pull together. I brought him up to speed on the latest problem with Lanier's firm backing out of the deal. He did not seem surprised. He explained to me that not many lawyers would invest in a case of this magnitude. It could cost many millions of dollars and take ten years or more to finally resolve.

He mentioned to me that he would run the case by Ron Motley's firm. Ron was the famous lawyer who took down big tobacco. Bruce happened to be married to one of the partners at the Motley Rice law firm headquartered out of Charlestown, South Carolina. Because of their relationship, our firm had been teaming together on some recent cases with Ron Motley's firm. Bruce Mattock said he would run the case by them and see if there was any interest.

Bruce soon reported back that they were interested. At least, it seemed as though one of the more senior partners was interested in the case. We scheduled a conference call to discuss the case with some of the lawyers tasked to investigate the case. They went over many of the same issues asked by the Lanier firm. However, the tone was quite different. They told me that they had a past case with the NFL that went very badly. It was a case involving an agent and player-related matter. I quickly told them that this case didn't involve any issues surrounding the CBA or current players. My case was drafted much like the successful cases involving Korey Stringer and Orlando Brown. I could immediately tell that these lawyers were going to be a tough sell on this lawsuit. I was ready for the challenge.

After I answered all of their questions, they next asked if they could meet one of the potential plaintiffs. I then flew out to meet with one of the players I had gotten to know in Sacramento, California. The meeting went well. The player was steadfast in suing the NFL. The young lawyer from Motley Rice asked all the right questions.

When the meeting was over, I drove back to the airport with the young lawyer. He expressed his concern over some facts that surrounded this particular plaintiff, like the fact that he only played two years in the NFL. He was concerned that the player had other prior concussions. I told him that there are plenty of other guys that would fit into his criteria that he is looking for in a plaintiff. I explained that this was not a case for one guy. There were hundreds of others just like this former player.

Regardless of our positive meeting, I expected to hear back from them that Motley Rice was not interested. Of course, I got that e-mail. It simply stated that they would tell the player that they will not represent him and that they wished me great luck and success with all of my NFL cases. Then I thought about who to approach next for a while and came up with another law firm to call. I had met some lawyers at Zimmerman Reed. They were a Minnesota class-action law firm that was working on a publicity rights lawsuit on behalf of the retired players. I had met some of their lawyers at the Summit in Las Vegas. I reached out to them by e-mail.

They responded quickly with interest. They asked for memorandums, factual information, and even a copy of the complaint that I had drafted. After a few weeks of discussing the case by e-mail with Zimmerman Reed, I received a response from them that "our group has decided not to actively pursue an action on the personal injury front at this time. We have looked extensively at these issues and currently believe the state of the law makes it very difficult to develop a theory of liability that would be viable against the NFL. We may decide to take another look at the case as time progresses and will be in touch if we decide to revisit the issue." Not surprisingly, from what I learned about lawyers and this case, Zimmerman Reed not only revisited the issue after I put this together, but they also got appointed to the steering committee on this case, which is an important leadership committee.

These statements became the recurring theme song of my phone calls to many lawyers. I next went after the law firm of Kline & Spector out of Philadelphia. Shanin Spector had resolved a case against LaSalle University on behalf of football player injured due to the second impact syndrome for many millions of dollars. I figured they would be interested. However, Mr. Spector's comments to me were that he would probably regret this decision, but he did not see how we could establish that the NFL was the cause of their head injury. I explained the injury is total and cumulative as was explained to me by Dr. Omalu, and the trauma induced in the NFL was a substantial contributing factor. Mr. Spector said that he did not like that theory of causation and would decline.

Mr. Spector did put me in touch with Alan Schwarz. Alan Schwarz is a Pulitzer Prize-nominated journalist from the New York Times who authored over 100 articles on the concussion issue relating to the NFL. He was one of the earliest journalists that exposed the concussion issue among football players off all ages. I was thrilled to be able to speak with him. He was one of the most knowledge-able people on this issue, and he had talked to everyone in the know about the concussion issue.

I introduced myself to Mr. Schwarz and told him that I was going to file a massive case against the NFL on behalf of many for-mer players. He instantly told me that there was no case. I could not believe he said that. How could he claim the title of being the guy that unmasked the concussion problem in football and not believe that there was a legal problem? I instantly put up my guard and defended my case. I explained what I had uncovered. After hearing me out, he said that there may be a case for a few guys who played recently, but I don't see you getting anywhere with the lawsuit against the NFL. I told him that I would file it and he could cover it if he wanted.

My phone calls, however, continued with other lawyers with who I was familiar. After a dozen similar messages that included good luck and not at this time, I next went to making cold phone calls. Those calls were met with the common theme of, "We will get back to you." They never did.

I was very frustrated. I spent nearly every free moment in 2010 trying to piece together a team to file this lawsuit, and I could not find a single lawyer in this country who had the guts to take on the NFL. I could not believe how many rejections I had gotten. It was unreal to think that lawyers who, by nature, were designed to cor-rect wrongs in society and deliver justice were more concerned with making money. No wonder our profession was losing its credibility.

During this time, Jack Tierney would consistently send me more legal cases to support what we were trying to do. Jack would always call with excitement in his voice, quoting opinions that he located and stating how the NFL case was similar to it. I would end up in his office sometimes to chat about a matter, and there would be seven copies of the same case.

Jack would always lift my spirits about finding a lawyer to team up with on the case. Toward the end of 2010, he asked how the search was going. I told him everything I had been through. I told him that I was not ready for my next rejection quite yet. He said to me that I should call the guys who did the McDuffie case. I told Jack that I could not handle another rejection around the Thanksgiving and Christmas holidays. I told him if he wanted to experience what it is like to go ahead and make the call himself.

CHAPTER 24

Jack's Call to Russomanno & Borrello

I should have known better. Jack took my response as a sign that he was allowed to make the call. Jack Tierney called over to the firm of Russomanno & Borrello in Miami, Florida, and spoke at length with Robert Borrello. He was very interested and wanted to set up a call with Herman Russomanno, who managed the firm. Jack told me the news which, at first, I thought he was joking. Nonetheless, we set up the next call immediately.

Russomanno & Borrello were coming off of a high in the legal system by winning a jury verdict for OJ McDuffie against the team physician for the Miami Dolphins. OJ McDuffie was a wide receiver taken in the first round out of Penn State University in 1993 by the Miami Dolphins. He ended up playing 116 career games for the Miami Dolphins. He ultimately retired in 2000 from a nagging toe injury. Earlier that year, Herman and Bob won a medical malpractice lawsuit related to OJ's career-ending toe injury. A jury ordered the former Dolphins team physician, Dr. John Uribe, to pay McDuffie $11.5 million in damages. The lawsuit alleged that Dr. Urbie told McDuffie to continue playing and that there was no damage to his toe despite the fact that MRI images showed otherwise.

Herman Russomanno and Robert Borrello may be the two kindest people I have ever met in this profession. They were both Italian and Catholic. They also were extremely professional, patient, personable, and thoughtful. I learned that they spent most of their time handling cases for severely injured people. The rest of their time was spent representing Donald Trump in his business dealings throughout the state of Florida. That was quite a diversity of a small practice. However, it gave them a very unique perspective from both sides of civil litigation.

Both Herman and I carried the conversation of the next telephone call. It was a productive meeting. They were interested in analyzing the legal issues surrounding the case. They were not fearful at all as to the defendant. They were more interested in whether there was a legal problem that required help. It was the first time that I saw lawyers look at the case from that perspective.

Reflecting on that first phone call, it was obvious that these two lawyers were not intimidated by names or size. After all, they represented the person who would be elected the next President of the United States. This led me to do further investigation of both Herman and Bob's backgrounds.

I started with Robert Borrello's background. He graduated with honors from the University of Miami School of Law. He was rated highly in the lawyer review associations. Most impressively, his strength was as a writer. He had dozens of significant appeals that were crafted into decisions of higher courts.

Herman Russomanno was as big of a lawyer as they had in the State of Florida. He was a past president of the Florida Bar and the Florida trial lawyers. He was on the American Bar Association Ethics Commission. This is the committee that writes the rules as to proper conduct that all lawyers must follow. He also was a member of the International Academy of Trial Lawyers. His practice led him to be awarded one of the Best Lawyer in America.

Herman and Bob spent a considerable amount of time poring over the memorandum, articles, documents, summaries, outlines, materials, case law, and medical documents that Jack and I shared with them. They kept asking for more materials, and we complied.

Every few days, it seemed as though Bob Borrello would call into our office and ask a few questions. Typically, they were questions about facts as they related to the NFL's actions, inactions, or the players specifically. They would pore over the collective bargaining agreements, the disability plans, and player contracts. Herman and Bob always had thoughtful questions.

After months and months of going over this information, they finally confirmed that they wanted to team up on this case. I could not even describe to you the joy that it brought to have high caliber lawyers team up on this case. I was once again excited that all this effort was finally going to pay off. However, there was one slight problem. They wanted to explore where this case needed filed as there was a possibility that it needed filed in a state where neither of our law firms were licensed.

Robert Borrello also had a number of legal questions that we needed to resolve before we could select the court to file this historic lawsuit. One of the first questions was whether this case was, in fact, a class action. A class action requires that there would be common issues of fact and law. The group must be so large that individual lawsuit would be impractical and that the claims or defenses in the cases must be typical of the plaintiffs and defendants. We analyzed in great detail this issue. It was clear that the damages suffered by the players were so different. Some had mild symptoms of brain injuries and were still functional in large part. Others were totally debilitated. Then there were those who died from CTE. It was clear that the damages would be extremely different. The second problem with declaring this case as a class action was that the group of retired players was discoverable. It could easily be determined how many and who those guys were that are living. The third problem with the class action was that the players played at different periods of time and for varying lengths of time. We believed that this was an important defense that would be raised by the NFL as to whether their league or some other source caused the player's brain injury.

Based on this analysis, Jack, Bob, and I agreed that a class action was not appropriate for this lawsuit. Rather, it would be yet another legal hurdle to a case filled with a number of legal hurdles we already expected.

Bob then asked questions about statutes of limitations and which state's law would apply based on where the NFL and Riddell were located. Concerning the issue of statute of limitations, the law generally requires a person to file a lawsuit within two years of his injury. Some states toll that period of time to when you discover the injury and its source. Other states require you to find out the source of who caused the injury. Concerning the issue of which state would apply their laws, the laws vary between different states based typically on which state has the most contacts to the case, the location of the injury, or the parties. This can be a rather complicated balancing test to figure out where is the appropriate state to file the lawsuit.

After all those issues were thoroughly discussed, Bob would then ask about other potential defendants. For instance, he wanted to know whether the teams should also be sued. I explained that the remedy against the teams were the workers compensation system. Further, the facts showed that the league undertook the duty to assess the concussion issue through creation of the mild traumatic brain injury committee and creating league-wide rules and safety committees.

He also asked about suing team physicians and trainers. After all, that was his specialty since he just had a successful result on behalf of OJ McDuffie. I explained that this issue would play to the strength of the NFL argument that the concussion matters were individualized team concerns. Bob agreed with my analysis.

Bob Borrello wanted to know more about the relationship of the NFL Players Association. He wanted to know whether they should be considered as someone to sue in this case. We talked at great length about this issue. I explained that the backdrop of the collective bargaining agreement was that the players association were chief negotiators. If we were to sue them, again, it would play right into the hands of the NFL that this issue was a matter of negotiations and that the players association dropped the ball by not giving it the attention that it deserved. Once again, this would be a deflection of the true problem created and disguised by the league. We agreed not to go that route either.

After we had thoroughly analyzed all of the legal issues, we scheduled a call with Jack, Bob, Herman, and me to discuss the next step. We had narrowed potential possible locations to file a lawsuit. Herman had two lawyers in mind with whom to discuss the case. He ultimately scheduled a conference call with the guy in California.

CHAPTER 25

Bringing in Tom Girardi

We set up a conference call with some lawyer in California. We did this because we felt that the case needed to be filed in California. By now, I was becoming robotic in explaining the case to others. Herman and Bob had arranged the call with the lawyer's secretary. I simply assumed that he was just a guy that would be our local contact to the state of California. I assumed that he would be nothing more than a drop box to help us file papers. Herman briefly introduced each of us on the call and then asked that I explain the backdrop of the case to the lawyer.

I went through step by exhausting step the facts surrounding the NFL. I talked about the players cognitive and functional injuries. I moved into the legal claims and the link to California. I explained what the lawsuit would allege against the NFL and Riddell.

The lawyer did not ask many questions. I assumed that he was either just learning the case, he was disinterested, or possibly he already had a handshake agreement with Herman to help be our local lawyer.

The call ended after I was finished. I asked if he had any questions. He said no and said that he would be back with us shortly. I left scratching my head. The lawyer certainly seemed very nice and polite. He also spoke very well. Something to me just did not seem right.

I asked Herman for his name and figured that I would look into this guy. I was never good with remembering names. Lo and behold, it was not hard to find a ton of information on Tom Girardi. Tom was one of the most distinguished and famous lawyers in the entire country. His practice was located in Los Angeles, California. His firm had around twenty-five lawyers. They all had prolific backgrounds and great success after attending highly ranked law schools.

The Girardi Keese Law Firm was designed to solely help injured persons, much like my law firm of Goldberg, Persky & White. Their cases mixed into anti-trust matters, defective drugs, and large wrongful death cases. The thing that amazed me though was the cases seemed to be high-profile cases with significant results, some in the many multi-millions of dollars.

I then had to figure out who was this Tom Girardi. He must be pretty big if he employed twenty-five lawyers. I was then stunned that I did not recognize who he was. Tom Girardi has obtained nearly thirty verdicts of over one million dollars. If a lawyer in his career ever obtains one verdict in excess of one million dollars, he was a good lawyer. To have two verdicts, then that person is a great lawyer. Tom was in a category by his lonesome.

If verdicts were not enough to discuss, he also had astronomical amounts of large settlements. A few cases involving consumer fraud were in the billions of dollars. Then I came across his settlement exceeding $300 million against Pacific Gas and Electric for injuring 650 residents in Hinkley, California. This case was made famous in the movie *Erin Brockovich*. I could not believe it. I was now working with the *Erin Brockovich* lawyer, and I just explained the case to him on a conference call as if he just started attending law school.

Tom Girardi was recognized as one of the nation's top trial lawyers. His resume alone was dozens of pages in length. I found out further information about Tom. He had connections with prominent people. He owned private jets. He is married to a singer on the billboard charts. He is friends with celebrities and major business figures. He owns hotels and restaurants in Las Vegas and Los Angeles. His close friend is former President Bill Clinton. His wife is featured in *The Real Housewives of Beverly Hills*.

I was excited at the prospect of working with a lawyer of Tom's caliber. I say this without taking anything away from Herman or some of the other lawyers I have previously mentioned. However, Tom was capable of taking this case on himself and not being financially strapped. He was powerful enough and connected enough to not be intimated by the NFL or its power.

After I researched Tom, I was eager to hear if he was going to join our team. I called and messaged Herman and Bob almost every day. I couldn't wait to hear if this guy would join up on this huge case. It would bring instant credibility to our lawsuit and a formidable team to represent all the injured players. We would have the trial lawyers, lawyers with financial backing, lawyers with writing ability and, of course, me with my connections, knowledge of the case, and contacts critical to the case.

A couple of weeks after that initial phone call, Tom sent a letter to Herman and Bob. I soon learned that the letters would be Tom's common method of communicating to us. He was an incredibly busy lawyer and businessman. He often would not make it to scheduled conference calls because he was triple booked. His letter stated that he had a team of lawyers and medical experts reviewing all the materials we had shared with him and that he would be back with us shortly.

More time passed, I was so excited to hear if this lawyer would join our team. Then we received another letter e-mailed by Tom's assistant. It said he would be back with us soon as he was meeting with some neuropsychologists to review the case with them. At this point, I was at least happy to hear that he was not running away like the other lawyers.

I was never concerned that another lawyer would try to do this case. It was apparent from my contacts with countless lawyers that there was too much risk and fear on the part of lawyers. The standard speech at the lawyer's conferences is that no one ever wants to be the first penguin in a new area of litigation. The first penguin who jumps in the water is the one who doesn't survive. Therefore, if I got Girardi on my team, it would give the appearance that this case was a real problem for the league. It would also make the former players feel comfortable that serious and experienced trial lawyers were fighting for them and their brain disease.

We soon heard back from Tom's assistant that he wanted to set up a conference call. I was excited to hear what he had to say. We all got on the call, including Jack, Herman, Bob, and me. Tom instantly assumed the ranks as the leader from this point forward. He quickly said that he was all in on this case. He was going to lead us. He told me to go get the players ready to file and keep editing the complaint and send to him to review it. He said this was very exciting, but we needed to carefully handle this delicate case. We could lose quickly on this preemption issue. However, if we prevailed on that issue, he liked our chances of great success.

I left the call thinking two things. It was finally going to happen. I better sign up as many players as I could find to join this case. By the way, where did I put that draft complaint? It is time to put it all together again.

CHAPTER 26

We are Ready to file, but the Players' Strike

As we entered early 2011, I had many contacts in the world of former NFL players. My name got around as well. Two of my original plaintiffs were becoming incredibly close to me. They would call my cellphone nearly every day to discuss the case. I think there were a number of reasons they got so involved with me.

I believe they felt disconnected from the league. I believe their brain injury caused them paranoia. I believe they needed a friend and an acquaintance who actually cared about them. I think they were curious in the law. Finally, I think they wanted to win, which would help all the guys.

These two guys, Vernon Maxwell and Rick Jones, would call and ask about the case. They would ask about my conversations with my team of lawyers. They would ask about my friendship and relationship with the experts. They would ask about my ability to handle the NFL's defenses. They would ask any question you could imagine. For me, it was therapeutic and practice for someday in the future when I would have to face all of these questions in the court. They, in turn, served as my sounding board to hear my case. They also served as practice for those days I would be asked questions about the case from others.

After the Moses conversation, a few clients, and I became even closer. We would text. We would share ideas about how to handle the case. They would discuss those difficult elephant in the room like issues about the case. They would ask if I really understood what I was on the verge of doing. They would ask if I understood what a big deal this case was going to be. They would ask if I understood how powerful the NFL was. I would always tell them yes. I did not want those unimportant factors to cloud my position on a legal issue. This was a matter of doing right and vindicating the name of my friend, Dr. Omalu, and helping these players and families. I could not worry about what the NFL would do to us or this case. I wasn't concerned about the attention it would bring to me. This case, and none of my cases, have ever been about me.

I was concerned about finding more players to join. I needed to let them know that there was a lawsuit that we were going to file. I learned that the retired player's association had lists of former players that contained e-mail addresses. A few of my clients helped by sending the players an e-mail that they were going to file a lawsuit with their lawyer and they should look into it.

My phone instantly began to ring non-stop. The players wanted information on the specifics. What were we looking to get? What were the risks? I explained that a case like this one is all contingent on success. Like the advertisements say, we get nothing unless you get something. At that point, we would seek 40 percent of a total recovery. This fee is standard in the practice of cases of this magnitude with a high risk and uncertain reward outcome. The players were concerned about suing the league that made them. When I started to get a few contracts signed, it was easy to say, "Well, I hope you do not miss out on what these other players signed."

Ultimately, my marketing strategy of convincing them to sign worked. I told them that a case like this required strength in numbers. The more injured guys, the better the case was, and it put more pressure on the league. I told them that when I hung up, they should call three of their friends and give them my cellphone number. This multiplication also worked. By the end of one call, I would often have two or three new voicemails.

In the meantime, I was working on editing the complaint. Every instance that I added a new player, it changed the entire formatting and paragraphing of the entire complaint. I would have to re-alphabetize the guys in the complaint. I would then have to put two other paragraphs in the body of the complaint so that it would identify specifically who the player was. After all, there has been a large number of Johnsons who played in the NFL.

My hometown Steelers were doing very well that season. They finished the regular season with twelve wins. They went on to the playoffs and squeaked away key wins against the Ravens and Jets to advance to Super Bowl XLV in Dallas, Texas. My same group of golf friends decided to take another super bowl trip, and we also included one additional friend, as our fourth.

This was quite a different experience in Dallas. We landed to an abnormal icy and cold front in the Texas region. We were stunned that the festivities were spread in different parts of the region as opposed to the centralized party in Tampa during the last Steeler's victory. I decided to pick up a virus and spend parts of the first two days sitting in our rented house. By game day, everyone was excited for a seventh super bowl championship. However, the game ended with a Steeler's loss. A couple of miscues, and quickly, the game and championship were in the hands of the Green Bay Packers.

I came home to learn that the league and players were threatening to strike and lock-out indefinitely. The last version of the collective bargaining agreement was set to end. It was yet another fight over the share of the growing revenues between the owners and the current players.

Our team agreed that we could not file the lawsuit quite yet. We figured that it would be an unforeseen obstacle that would hold up football. We never wanted this case to be an end of the game of football. It needed to be a case that the fans, and particularly the parents of football players, supported. They need to understand that we are not anti-football; rather, we are pro-athlete. Therefore, the concussion lawsuit was once again on lock-out, just like the players.

Going back in time, as much as a fan that I had been of sports and football, in general, I never would have thought that would be the last game of football that I would ever watch. The adventure of chasing this case had created a full-time job for me. My life became football. My free time became football. I no longer wanted my hobby and spare time to be watching football games.

I could not get away from football. Everywhere I turned, I was asked questions about the case. Every lawyer I ran into wanted to know about it. My family always asked how the case was going. Then my phone and e-mail was always tying up my time. I couldn't spend an evening in peace after my daughters went to bed without my phone ringing. They couldn't wait for their calls to be returned. Because of their brain symptoms, they would keep calling and calling until they spoke with me directly at that moment in time. Then, when I got to the golf course to enjoy some free time, my friends would ask me about it. It was too much football for me. I no longer have time for the games.

While on lockout, there was a concern that the 2011 season could be wiped away. They may hold out an entire year. As much as a hardship it would have been on the players, it was a greater hardship on my emotions. I was ready to go. However, we were on a timeout.

CHAPTER 27

It's Time to File—
What Stays in

It finally appeared as though the lockout and strike were going to end in July. The media was reporting that it could happen and there would be a shortened training camp. We quickly set up a conference call with Herman, Bob, Jack, Tom Girardi, and me. The conversation was whether we should wait until the CBA was signed to file or not.

Jack, in the meantime, had done some research which he believed showed that the NFL was more likely to lose the preemption argument if we filed the case during their lockout. He believed some case law showed that if there is no CBA in existence, then the NFL could not argue labor preemption. He was excited about this issue. In fact, he was able to get Herman, Bob, and I to buy into this argument, and he had our vote in favor of filing before there was a newly signed CBA.

On our conference call, Tom Girardi, however, was pretty adamant that we should wait patiently until the new CBA was signed. He was concerned that a case like this could hijack them getting a deal done with respect to the CBA. Then we would ultimately look like the bad-guy lawyers who were holding up NFL football from the fans. We were very strongly in support of filing by now. With the pressure from Herman, Bob, Jack, and I, Tom ultimately gave in to agreeing to file. It was a Thursday when we had this phone call. He said that we would file the case on Monday. It would be filed very quietly. There would be no press conferences or publicity. When it leaked, we would be confident and stand firm on our position with this case. He encouraged us not to be afraid of speaking with the media.

Before the call ended, Tom asked me to sign up as many players as possible and get the complaint to him on Monday morning for final edits. I asked what legal claims should go in the case, and he said we should allege everything.

I left that call so excited. The big day was only a few days away. Then I got very nervous. The discussions about media for the first time frightened me. Maybe I wasn't ready for the big time. I was doing just fine with the job I had. I know my wife, Kelly, did not want the stress and conflict this case could bring to our lives.

I did not have time to worry about this issue. I needed to finalize the names of all the guys who were going to create history by suing the NFL for their cover-up of brain damaged players. After another e-mail was sent around to the NFL retirees, my phone again started to explode. I told players that this was going to, at some point, gain media attention. They needed to be brave and ready for the attention that it would bring. If they had cold feet, they should not join this lawsuit. I was clear that, by joining this case, they were agreeing to sue the NFL, NFL Properties, and Riddell, and that it would all be contingent upon our success.

Former player after former player called me non-stop from Friday until Monday morning. In between calls and voice mails, I was working on putting the final touches on the complaint. I didn't have time to have others working on it. It would have been too many cooks in the kitchen. I handled everything during those critical moments except for a few calls that I passed on to Jack to allow me a few breaks in time.

The final version of the complaint included one very important legal term. It was the word that I spelled incorrectly in elementary school spelling bee—"fraud." Fraud was a separate legal claim in a civil action that required a person to prove that there was a false statement of fact, knowledge that the defendant knew it was untrue, intent to deceive, reliance on the part of the person suing, as well as injuries to that person. The NFL committed fraud by lying about concussions to the players, and they knowingly took those statements to mean that they were not injured and continued to play the game with brain injuries. The NFL denied and contested the allegations of fraud throughout the entirety of the litigation and pleadings.

This was the critical piece to the case that separated it from *Stringer* and *Brown*. We no longer had just a negligence case against the NFL. This was something that was way outside of collective bargaining or their negotiation process. Since the NFL had superior knowledge on brain trauma, they could not defraud the guys playing the sport regarding this issue of latent brain diseases from playing football. It was our dagger in the heart of the NFL to prevail on this case. It was as basic as the pigskin is to the game.

In the meantime, Jack Tierney had also crafted another legal claim that was unique to our final complaint. It correlated to the *Orlando Brown* court decision. Jack found some case law in some old anti-trust cases that showed that a company who holds a monopoly owes a duty of safety to the public. He argued that the NFL was a monopolist. In fact, when the USFL sued the NFL, the court determined that the NFL was, in fact, a monopoly. This lawsuit involved the unfair actions of the NFL to overpower and shutdown the other professional football league that was trying to operate as a competitor in the 1980s. We argued that the NFL was a monopoly and controlled the game of football. For instance, they created the NFL *Play 60,* teaching kids how to properly play the game of football. These actions made them the authority on the game of football. Every league copied the NFL's model for rules, gameplay, and safety.

In their capacity as a monopoly, the NFL owed a duty of care to not only their league but the public at large. Parents, amateur athletes, doctors, and children relied on the information the NFL produced as the most reliable and best information on the subject, whatever the subject was. Here, however, the NFL set forth bad science. They misled everyone on the issue of concussion, CTE, and football. Therefore, the NFL breached their duty of care to the public at large.

With inclusion of the fraud claim and the negligence as a monopolist claim, I felt that the complaint was stronger that the

Stringer and *Brown* cases against the NFL. I felt like we had a solid case that would get us past the preemption argument.

The country would soon understand that the NFL did not properly evaluate and teach players about brain injury problems. They failed to perform any baseline testing of the players. They failed to make any medical diagnoses of concussions or concussion symptoms. They did not offer treatments for brain injuries. They did not educate the players on identifying signs and symptoms of a concussion. Lastly, they failed to offer any return to play guidelines or protocol much like the National Hockey League had created in the early 1990s.

As each former player called and signed my contingent retainer agreement, my formatting and paragraphs of the complaint would need renumbering to add them to the complaint. It was almost impossible to keep up with this over the busy weekend. I sat in my basement with my computer and phone attached to me. On Monday morning, I went into the office with plans to e-mail the final version of the complaint to everyone by 11:00 a.m. so that any final edits could be made, and it would be filed that day. I did just that after getting in the office around 4:00 a.m. to work on my additions.

There were very few edits to the complaint. There were some grammatical changes and some mistakes with the playing careers of the players. Overall, it was my proudest written work as a lawyer.

It was ultimately in Tom's hands after Bob's edits by noon, which would have been 9:00 a.m. in California. I expected that Tom Girardi would quietly file and send us a cover sheet with a docket number illustrating that it was filed.

Jack, Bob, and I were completely anxious to hear that it was filed. Between the three of us, we must have called and e-mailed dozens of times to Tom's assistant on that day. We never heard anything back on Monday, July 18, 2011. In the meantime, I kept getting a few more latecomers that wanted to get on the complaint.

The next morning, I called Robert Borrello to inquire if he heard whether the lawsuit was filed. He did not hear anything from Girardi's office. I told him that I ought to add these few new guys to the draft complaint and resend over to Tom's office this morning. Bob agreed with this strategy.

We then called over to Girardi's office to inquire whether it was filed. No one seemed to have the answer. We then decided to tell them that if it was not filed yesterday, then they should please file this newer version that adds a couple of new names.

I made sure that every person on this list was diagnosed or had significant symptoms identified with CTE. We all agreed that a lawsuit should not be brought for any players who were not injured or symptomatic. Therefore, there were dozens of callers that I had to tell who we could not help at this time due to the fact that they were currently fine from a cognitive and brain functional capacity.

It was now Tuesday, July 19, 2011, and we waited to hear confirmation of whether the lawsuit was filed by Girardi's office. The day went by with numerous calls and e-mails to Girardi and his assistant. I had no idea whether it was filed or not.

I woke up the next morning to begin my routine of working out in my basement. I usually do some treadmill, stationary biking, and weights. Now, I cycle daily every morning and have completed seven century rides. It has been my escape from the world around me as I get to be outdoors and listen to music while riding before the world awakens.

On the morning of July 20, I went down to my basement and turned on ESPN Sportscenter while I started my work out. Immediately, I looked at the scrolling screen to see the scores, stats, and results of yesterday's baseball games. Then it came across the screen. "75 former players are suing the NFL, claiming the league intentionally withheld knowledge of the damaging effects of concussions for 90 years." The shock and emotions struck me at 5:00 a.m. like you could not imagine. I stopped instantly and ran upstairs to tell Kelly. My world and, soon, the entire world, would change because of this filing.

We had just filed the case that Alan Schwartz once wrote that the NFL feared most. They feared individual lawsuits as opposed to a class action. The National Football League was on pace to soon have to defend hundreds of claims made by former players on a case-by-case basis.

CHAPTER 28

Reactions

The news of this major lawsuit was broken by TMZ. TMZ is the celebrity tabloid news source that typically covers gossip surrounding Hollywood's actors and actresses. Apparently, they have an employee who searches the daily filings in Los Angeles state courthouse. By the end of the day, they noticed that a massive case was filed against the NFL. They reported that seventy-five players filed a lawsuit against the NFL. They reported the case alleged that the NFL knew as early as the 1920s of the harmful effects on a player's brain of concussions. However, the NFL concealed these facts from coaches, trainers, players, and the public. They reported the case was being led by Mark Duper, Otis Anderson, and Rodney Hampton.

I figured that I would soon walk into the office with a million requests for interviews. I walked into the office and there was very little press coverage. It hit a few newspapers, but the national media did not cover the filing of it. However, the one thing that was clear was that this case brought with it hostilities.

The NFL quickly responded thorough league spokesman Greg Aiello issuing a statement saying the NFL has not "seen the complaint but would vigorously contest any claims of this kind." It seemed that the public and media were going to echo those NFL statements. It fueled serious emotions that included threats of harm to me. The common off-the-cuff comments were that the players knew better and this was nothing more than a money grab.

Halfway through the day, I received a request to do an interview on CNN with one of my clients. Joe Harris was a former linebacker that played on various teams. He was the epitome of this case. He was an above-average player that played more than five NFL seasons. He played in a Super Bowl. He never received a contract of a hundred thousand dollars let alone one million dollars. In his fifties, he was suffering from CTE symptoms and early onset dementia.

Joe was taken to the Atlanta studios by limousine to do the live interview. I, in turn, was asked to participate by telephone. It was clear from the first question that this was going to be a difficult interview. I was not the least bit concerned. Joe and I were prepared for these questions. My only concern was whether he could recall everything we discussed.

The reporter asked Joe why he joined the lawsuit. What was the lawsuit about? What did the NFL do wrong? What did he want to get out of the lawsuit? Didn't he know better that football could cause brain injuries?

Joe was unbelievable. He talked about the NFL never being there for the former players. He talked about the NFL not sharing with them information on brain injuries so they could make informed decisions. He explained that this lawsuit was designed to educate future generations of children so that they did not have the problems of these older guys. He explained that football was a great game, but they never were told that they signed up for later-life brain problems.

They only asked me one question about why the wives joined the lawsuit. I explained how they have a claim for their loss of consortium and they were damaged as much as their husbands and have become their caretakers.

It was the first interview for this case and was a great success. I quickly posted the interview on our law firm's website and shared it with all of the players who were clients. I told them they should use Joe's interview as a guide to handling interviews in this case. I was proud of Joe. He exceeded my expectations. The players sent him numerous congratulatory notes and messages.

By the end of the day, there were a couple of interview requests from much smaller sources. All in all, it was a quiet day except for the negative messages in response to the print articles on the internet.

The attention from filing the lawsuit did cause many new clients to call my phone wanting to join the lawsuit. My phone again seemed to pick up in the number of calls after the public announced the filing of our original NFL lawsuit.

The next day arose with a new problem. I received a call from one of Otis Anderson's publicists asking about the lawsuit. I told them the same things about the lawsuit that was discussed with every person. I told them Otis Anderson knowingly joined our lawsuit. By the end of the afternoon, they went to the media and released a statement stating that Anderson spoke to my law firm once but never agreed to be involved in the suit and was surprised to see his name on it. "As the New York alumni chapter's former president, my concern is with the players," Anderson said. "I think there are more constructive ways of finding solutions to the issues we face than litigation."

I quickly had to go into damage control. I was stunned that a former player would spit at his own brothers by jumping out of the case at a critical time. These actions made all of my clients look like they were not for real.

This situation caused some public relations concerns. It also caused some of the plaintiffs to reconsider whether they should have joined this lawsuit. I reassured them that the dust storm would blow over and that this case would be fought in the court of law. They simply could ignore the media and their requests and let us fight this case in court.

The next interesting story with the media involved an interview on ESPN radio where they explored all of those difficult subjects surrounding the allegations in the lawsuit. I was prepared beyond belief. They were ready to talk about players knowing better. They thought these guys were multi-millionaires. I told them about the $40,000 per year non-guaranteed contracts. I educated them on the lack of pensions. Then they finally thought they would corner me and end the interview on how lawyers are the scum of society and sue everyone for any little thing.

They ended the show by asking about whether I am just going to start suing the NHL and other sports leagues. I responded that it was funny they brought that up. I said that there would be no reason to sue anyone else unless they created a similar culture of defrauding the players of the dangers. If the NFL would have done what the NHL did for its players regarding concussions, we would not have a public health epidemic related to football concussions. I explained that, in the early 1990s, Eric Lindros and Pat Lafontaine retired due to post-concussions syndrome. At that time, the NHL took appropriate action and created concussion protocols and required the players to be released to return to play by independent physicians certified in brain injury. In comparison, the NFL covered up this issue after Steve Young and Troy Aikman retired and published fraudulent papers and science that contradicted ninety years of brain injury information known to the world. And that was the end of the interview. They were unable to poke a single hole into our lawsuit politically, morally, or socially. I again shared that interview with all of my clients to encourage them that we were on the right path for them.

Over the next week or two, there would be some more media requests, but nothing that was different or noteworthy. I was shocked that the national media was not touching this story. Maybe they were fearful of touching an issue that was adverse to the NFL that would risk falling out of their good graces. After all, their breads were all buttered by the NFL machine.

The other thing that happened was that more players started to come out of the woodwork. They were now discussing the case on the internet blogs and at their alumni meetings. They talked about their concussions. Many would talk about the hits they received on special teams which they used to call the suicide squad. They were starting to understand that there was a reason for their cognitive and functional symptoms. This led to many more guys calling to join the lawsuit. I was busy getting them on board for the next group to file suit.

The other significant thing that happened was doctors and experts would come out of everywhere, e-mailing and calling asking my assistants, Cindy DeUnger or Kim Siebert, whether they could speak directly with me because they had something important to discuss. Some claimed they had pills that could cure concussions. Others believed that they uncovered blood tests that could detect concussions. Others claimed that had the secret goods on the NFL's cover up of concussions. Others alleged that the players would heal if changing to a healthy lifestyle with organic compounds and vitamins. Then there were others that swore that hyperbaric oxygen therapy was replenishing lost and damaged brain cells. It became a full-time job handling and sifting through these inquiries.

There was also one other significant change that happened the same week that we filed our lawsuit. The NFL moved the kickoffs for the upcoming season from the thirty-yard line to the thirty-five-yard line. This would lead to less return attempts by the kicking team during the special teams play that lead to the most concussions during the collusions that occur during the kickoffs. It was an effort to reduce the number of concussions sustained on kickoffs. It was a subtle change not given much attention. However, I believe it was a change that came as a result of filing this damaging case. The timing said it all.

The other action that the NFL took when we filed the case was to ask one of our younger players to return to the league. This guy had recently retired as an offensive lineman. One of the teams has lost their starter and was in need of a replacement. They went right after my client. This resulted in the NFL's lawyers getting involved in an effort to attempt to have this player sign a waiver regarding the NFL lawsuit we just filed. They attempted to mislead this guy into signing a document that said that he did not have concussion-related symptoms and that he lied in the complaint filed with the court. Further, they tried to throw language in the document that prohibited the player from ever reentering the lawsuit.

I was not surprised that this happened after the Otis Anderson incident. These actions led to me receiving a call from the head of the active player's agents and player's association, asking that I tell my client not to sign the document because it would, in essence, be forced on all current players that they are now assuming the risk of head injuries. I told the agent not to worry, and I told my client not to sign the document unless he wants to be charged with defrauding a court of law. He did, however, leave the lawsuit in continued hopes of chasing his dream.

As much as we had a long road ahead to educate the media and public, based on these actions, it was clear the NFL was very concerned with my case, and they were doing whatever they could behind the scenes to mitigate the damage to their shield.

CHAPTER 29

The Sharks Arrive

I had daily conversations with the few players with whom I became close. My clients always posed the best questions. They were clearly invested in this matter. They did their homework by researching and speaking to many knowledgeable people.

One of my memorable conversations was concerning what could derail this case. I would typically respond by saying the pre-emption issue. However, one day, they were not satisfied with that answer. They wanted to know what could screw up this case. I told them that public perception could hurt. They still were not satisfied with that answer. They said that wives and parents would be the voices and face of this litigation. No one wanted their children to have brain injuries. Still not satisfied, they pushed on about what could hurt this case. I finally answered that the only thing that could change this case is if bad lawyers got involved.

This was the answer they wanted to discuss. How could bad lawyers hurt the case? How could any lawyer do this? I explained that I doubted that lawyers would ever join this lawsuit. No one wanted this case or believed in it. There were so many people that told me no. However, there always was the risk that lawyers would show their true colors and join the lawsuit if they sensed there was something financially in it for them.

The players still did not understand how some other lawyer could hurt this case. I explained that it took me years to research and analyze this case. I am on top of the facts, the law, the science, the medicine, and the preemption argument. I explained that since there is no copyright protection in the practice of law, a lawyer could simply swoop in and steal our work and sign up a few guys. Then he could file a case in some location and get a very bad ruling that the NFL could flash to our judge in their California case, and that would be the end for all of our efforts.

Regretfully, other lawyers would get involved in this case. It was almost impossible to believe that these same lawyers that said that there were concerns over every issue in the case and why they would not get involved jumped into this litigation. These lawyers had previously cited concerns over preemption, proof of causation from playing in the NFL, assumption of the risk, comparative negligence of the players, choice of law concerns as to what laws would apply, lack of standing, and even concerns of the fact that a class action could not be brought. They could care less that they didn't want involved upfront. They were ready to jump in now that they could stand in the shadows of Tom, Herman, and my law firm.

I was very naïve to the fact that they could actually take over the entire litigation. This biggest nightmare all started within weeks of filing our first case. By August 4, we had filed a second lawsuit. It was filed the day before the new 2011 Collective Bargaining Agreement was executed. This lawsuit was led by forty-seven players including the likes of Leonard Marshall, Dave Pear, and Hall-of-Famer Tony Dorsett.

However, around that time, I received a call from a lawyer in California that handled workers compensation cases for a number of former NFL players. He too had just recently started adding claims for their brain injuries as well as their other bodily injuries. He wanted to work with us on these cases. I quickly told him that he can refer us any client and we would take it from there. If he had any other questions, he could reach out directly to Tom Girardi and work out the referral agreement.

He was unsatisfied with this response. He wanted to work the cases up jointly. I quickly bit back and said that we were not interested in anyone joining our team. We didn't need their help on these cases. He could sit back and get a slice of the pie, if we win, by simply referring his NFL guys to us. He said that was insufficient, that he wanted to work on the cases.

I said, "Look, no one understands these cases, and we don't need anyone screwing them up." I told him that he could simply file his own lawsuit by stealing all of my work. The complaint is public record. I stated that I hope he wouldn't be that selfish to do such a thing, but I couldn't stop him from doing it.

A week later, he did just that. He filed a lawsuit for about ten former players, copying word for word everything that took me years and thousands upon thousands of hours of unpaid labor. It was even filed in the same court as our case.

A few weeks later, another lawsuit was filed. This time, it was filed in Philadelphia. This one was filed in federal court and included class action claims. Two issues that played directly in the hands of the NFL's defenses to win this case. I should have guessed at this point that these lawyers would be the beginning of the end of this litigation. They wanted to also make a big press splash. They even asked Dr. Omalu to go to a press conference to announce their filing of their lawsuit. The fourth case to be filed against the NFL regarding brain-damaged former players. Dr. Omalu swiftly refused when he found out they were not working with me despite trying to tell him otherwise.

As more time passed, I received calls from the lawyers at Zimmerman Reed. They asked for a copy of my complaint and wondered if I would meet with them in Minnesota. Something changed their mind. They were going to get involved, and they wanted to work with me.

Another law firm from Washington DC pestered me daily to speak to me about the lawsuit against the NFL. They too wanted to work with me. I kindly asked them to talk to Tom Girardi.

There were law firms in New York, Florida, Atlanta, and more in Philadelphia coming out of the woodwork and grabbing players to file my lawsuit with former players they signed up. All the while, they were telling players that they were working with me. Those that didn't lie to players in that way were relaying to the players that they were leading the case. Finally, those who did not like those two methods were offering a cheaper contingent fee percentage. It was easy to do that since I already did the work to figure out the case. Most egregious of all was direct solicitations that told the players to join on so they did not miss out on the settlement. What settlement? Could they really get away with that unethical behavior?

There were some very nice lawyers who joined this litigation and have always sincerely recognized my efforts on this case. For instance, there were the guys in Atlanta, Mike McGlamry and Bruce Hagen, who told players that they were only interested in guys who did not have lawyers. They also would state at retired players meetings in Georgia that I was the reason this case existed.

By December, there were lawyers throughout the country filing my concussion case in areas including Louisiana, California, and Texas. Players were completely confused as to who their lawyers were. They were signing on with multiple lawyers as each lawyer told them they needed to sign with them as their lawsuit was different. But they were not.

At one point, I suggested to Tom and Herman that we ought to try to discuss working together in some manner. They agreed. I sent an e-mail asking a number of these lawyers to talk. I was stunned at some of the responses. However, my favorite response was from a Philadelphia lawyer who replied, "Who are you and what lawsuit are you talking about?"

Regardless of these efforts, my clients would send me e-mails and tell me about the direct phone calls they would receive from lawyers and agents of lawyers who were well aware that they were represented by me. In the practice of law, it is completely unethical to contact a represented person to seek to represent them in the same case. Those types of actions are disciplinary by the bar up to and including loss of license. It is a taboo in the legal profession to attempt to steal another lawyer's client. These actions, however, became the start of common unethical and inappropriate conduct that I had predicted would ruin this monumental case that I poured my heart into.

I would ask myself how I could fight back. What should I do to respond and protect my clients? None of these lawyers had the talents, background, or results of Tom and Herman. Where were they when I was trying to pull this all together? I decided that the best strategic course to handle the lawyers was to simply promote our team for who we were. Our team is the guys who started it all. I listed our backgrounds and experience, and I concluded with stating that we were also suing Riddell. I could not figure out why the rest of these lawyers chose not to include Riddell. Then our secret weapon was that Dr. Omalu was my friend.

My team would not enter the fray of bad lawyering and wrongfully soliciting clients. There were even rumors going around at the time that some of these lawyers were paying players to find other players to sign up. This was the death knell of unethical lawyering. If someone found that out, you would lose your license to practice law or maybe even go to jail.

Tom Girardi was not too concerned. He was speaking at lawyer conferences all over the country. He told us that lawyers were coming up to him asking him if he would lead the NFL cases. He alleviated our fears that lawyers were going to squeeze us away from the case and our clients. Rather, it was just the opposite impression the lawyers gave him that they wanted him to lead the case.

The sharks were circling in the water sensing blood from my lawsuit. They must have sensed blood from my lawsuit. In August through November, there were over a thousand former players signed up and joining lawsuits identical to my original case in courthouses all over the country. They were all running to the press and shouting from the tallest trees to look at them.

CHAPTER 30

Lost Mom

While all of this was going on, my mom and dad were spending a lot time with our kids. They lived a short fifteen-minute ride to our house. My girls were going to be four and three in the summer of 2011. They were growing up fast and were already very active. From the time that our youngest, Alexis, was born, our oldest decided that she did not need to take any naps. Therefore, their days always seemed to be non-stop from 5:00 a.m. until about 7:00 p.m.

My mom was always begging us to go places so that she would be a babysitter. I think she had every plan imaginable of things and activities that they could do together while the parents were not there to be the voice of discipline. Kelly and I did get to go to a lot of dinners and hockey games during early 2011.

In late March 2011, we decided to do a family vacation. We had just taken a trip to Disneyworld in Orlando, Florida, the year before for the first time with the kids. We decided that a trip to other parks in Florida would be a fun trip to take with the kids, and this time, we were going to take my parents. We decided to stay at the Nickelodeon resort to be around the characters and go to Sea World and Universal. The last day was going to be at Chef Mickey Mouse's breakfast with the Disney characters, and then we would stop at Downtown Disney to do some shopping.

During that trip, it was rather noticeable that my mom was lagging behind us. She complained at night about pain and swelling that she was experiencing. She always stated that something was wrong with her stomach. None of the multiple doctors she visited could locate any problems of serious significance.

A month later, my mom was sent to have her back checked. They thought that maybe all of her problems were stemming from her back region. She had a CT scan of her back. The afternoon of the next day, she was called by her family doctor to tell that they found cancer in her stomach and it was bad.

I will never forget receiving the call from my mom. It was a nice Wednesday afternoon, and I went out to enjoy the best spring day of golf weather we had seen in 2011. Just when I turned to the tenth hole, I received the horrific call from my mom. It is the kind of phone call that you never want to receive from a loved one in your life.

In early May, she was diagnosed with metastatic gall bladder cancer. A very rare cancer with no known cause. She was sent to determine the full progression of her condition with additional tests. The tests determined that her cancer was untreatable. All they could do for her was pain management. She was given a matter of months to live.

This was a life-changing event for our family. Her mother was now going to outlive her and be the responsibility of my father, my brother, and I. Over the next few months, my mom continued to deteriorate. She withdrew from all of her social activities. She did not want to tell people about her diagnosis.

My brother was confused how such an event could get away from the doctors. After all, she had an ultrasound months ago to assess those types of problems. He then decided to have some of his physician friends review that ultrasound to determine whether the cancer was present nine months prior and whether it was treatable.

Those doctors reported back to my brother that it was a treatable cancer back then and that the radiologist missed the tumor on the CT scan. He said that I should double check this matter with one of the doctors who I have used over the years to read x-rays. I did the same, and it came back showing a failure to diagnose her cancer.

It was a rather difficult issue for us to decide whether to pursue a medical malpractice lawsuit. After all, my brother is a physician. It would require him to be involved in going after someone in his own profession in a medical malpractice lawsuit. Regardless, it came down to my mom determining that she wanted to file a lawsuit against this radiologist. She did not want another person to ever experience a similar outcome. Unfortunately, we learned that this was the third time this doctor had been sued for malpractice.

Once my mom decided that she wanted to sue the doctor, it was next to determine who should handle the case. I told her that I had a number of friends that handle these types of cases and do a good job. My concern was that they would not treat my mom's case personally. I feared that it would be just another medical malpractice file sitting on a shelf.

I told my mom that I could handle the case. After all, I had done a few of these medical malpractice cases in the past. What was so different about this one that I couldn't handle? I was getting ready to file the NFL case. This was a straight-forward lawsuit in comparison. However, my biggest concern was how I would handle a number of the difficult tasks, including videotaping my mom's deposition.

My family agreed that I should handle the case. My solution for the emotional parts of the case was to ask Pete Paladino to get involved. We filed my mom's lawsuit right after the NFL and Riddell case was filed in July. Pete quickly hurried to meet with my mom and worked on preparing her for the deposition.

My mom handled her deposition fantastically even though it was done in a hospice center in early October. She progressed so rapidly that she was unable to drive in August. In September, she was having difficulty doing anything. By October, she was unable to eat and taken to a hospice center. Toward the end of October, she asked to be taken back home. On October 27, she passed away with our family by her side.

My mom's case was ultimately put together by Todd and me. Pete offered important help with the emotional parts like my mom's deposition, the treating doctor's deposition, and my dad and brother's deposition. He offered another set of eyes to review documents and strategy. My brother was able to advise me step by step on the medical aspects of the case. I even had him sit next to me when I deposed the doctor who was sued. Needless to say, the defense counsel was up in arms about that tactic. When Todd was deposed, he was incredible. I think his deposition was the key moment of the case. It showed that they had an insurmountable case to win as a doctor and son was completely honest, sincere, intelligent, and also an expert with the medicine.

Over time, this lawsuit resolved under a confidential settlement. It offered no solace to replacing the loss we suffered. We believe that lawsuit will prevent the doctor who missed her diagnosis from ever having that happen again to another patient. There is not a day that goes by where I don't think about the loss our family endured. My kids lost the best grandmother in the planet. It caused our family to be broken up over this issue. We lost our closeness as my mom was the glue that held us all together during good and bad times.

My mom was always my motivation to succeed in all of my endeavors. It was her that taught me to never give up on my work or activities. I always feared failing to disappoint her and not living up to her expectations. I think she knew that the NFL case would turn out to be big.

It is sad when I think about how much she is missed. It sad to think that she has missed Addison's nutcracker ballet performances. She has missed Alexis riding her horse and golfing. She has missed vacations in Disneyworld. She has missed our home near the beach. She has and the way this case has changed my legal career and my growth as a lawyer and person.

My work occasionally takes me to areas near my hometown. It is during those occasions that I make sure to stop by the mausoleum where she rests peacefully. Those visits for me end up being reenergizing as it helps me feel invincible in those often insurmountable tasks and projects that I am facing.

The period of May through October of 2011 for me was more than just an NFL case. I would literally work non-stop on the NFL and leave work early to spend a few hours every afternoon with my mom. Then it would be off to home to a late night of catching up on what I missed. It was an indescribable emotional period in my life. It undoubtedly hardened me and changed me to be a tougher person.

I know my mom is in heaven watching this case from the stands cheering me on until the final minute of the game. I know she is proud of my efforts and my persistence. She was always my biggest fan. And, I know she appreciates the enormity of taking down an 800 pound gorilla with just a stone in my hand. My dad feels the same and assures me of these sentiments all the time.

CHAPTER 31

Meanwhile,
Our Pending Case

While all of these issues were going on, our first two lawsuits were removed to federal court in California by the NFL as expected. The NFL by right could remove the case arguing that the case involved a matter of federal law. In this case, it was the Labor Management Relations Act that they were arguing applied to this case.

Once the NFL took that affirmative step which we could not stop, and then it was our turn to file a motion to remand the case back to state court where we filed. We were prepared with that motion. Jack Tierney had spent a number of hours preparing a nice memorandum of law outlining the legal basis for sending the case back to state court.

We found out that the judge who was assigned to the case in federal court was Judge Manuel Real. He was born in 1924 to Spanish immigrant parents. He was appointed to the U.S. District Court for the Central District of California in 1966 by President Lyndon Johnson.

Judge Real had a knack for creating schedules that moved faster than any other judge who I have experienced. We had to move quickly and file our motion to remand. The NFL only had days to respond. Then it would be set for a quick oral argument.

Around this time, now that the legal work was facing us, Tom Girardi had one of his partners get involved to help on the litigation of this case. Graham LippSmith was the partner assigned to oversee the day to day NFL litigation matters from his office. He was a lot easier to locate when we had a matter that was urgent. He is a brilliant young lawyer with a ton of experience in high profile cases that Girardi's office handled.

He was the person who was tasked with arguing the pending motion to remand the case to state court. Prior to doing that, Jack and I put the final touches on our brief as to why the NFL did not have a right to have the NFL case heard in federal court. There were a number of bullet points, but the major issues were that this case mirrored *Stringer*. It also mirrored *Brown* in that the claims affected the public at large. We also argued that this case belonged in state court because the claims involved allegations of fraud which could not have been fairly negotiated by the parties. On top of that, the two strongest arguments left in the motion included, first, the fact that the guys were retirees. They were not parties to the collective bargaining process. Second, there was no collective bargaining agreement at the time we filed the lawsuit because the players were on strike and locked out.

We were prepared to win this landmark case. It was a matter of a state law action giving the federal court system no jurisdiction to assert over this case. The finishing touches on the brief were put on by Bob Borrello and Graham LippSmith.

Graham was scheduled to have this matter argued in front of Judge Real. He was prepared with all of the arguments. It was a courthouse that he had been in front of many of times. The argument lasted less than ten minutes. Neither side had an opportunity to speak, even though Graham had tried to interrupt the judge. Rather, Judge Real took the opportunity to review the case and state that he was maintaining jurisdiction over the case as one of the claims appeared very similar to the *Stringer* claim. In a few days, we received his opinion stating his thoughts that he stated days earlier from the bench.

His opinion relayed that the general negligence claim was very similar to the claim alleged in the *Stringer* case. In that case, the court found that a general negligence claim was too close to the collective bargaining agreement. In other words, the collective bargaining agreement needed to be interpreted to determine the roles and responsibilities of safety and health matters involving the players.

When we were deciding what to add to the complaint that was filed, one of the questions we continued to ponder was whether we should leave a general negligence claim in the complaint. It was a very difficult decision. I figured it gave a judge an easy out to claim that legal issues had been adjudicated in another past case in favor of the NFL. Unfortunately, my gut feeling was right on that issue. Tom Girardi, on the other hand, wanted it all in the case.

It therefore forced our next step that we anticipated in this case. The NFL would move to dismiss our lawsuit in its entirety. This was the bad news. The good news was that we still had strong arguments on the negligence monopoly and fraud claims against the league. The very good news was that the judge relayed that this case was similar to *Stringer*. This suggested to us that we could and should likely prevail against NFL Properties and Riddell. Riddell was taken to the verge of trial before settling with the Stringer family. It was a mixed bag at the moment. However, I did not have time to deal with Monday morning quarterbacking. I had to prepare our response to the NFL's motion to dismiss.

The NFL's motion to dismiss was due on December 20. Based on Judge Real's rocket schedule, it made our response due on December 27. This was not the way that I was looking forward to spending my Christmas with my four and three year old. Not to mention it was not how I wanted to spend my first Christmas without my mom. However, it did offer me an opportunity to take my mind off of thinking about our loss. I know that my mom would want me to be successful on this case.

There was a page limit on the length of our response. I did my best to capture those strong arguments, up front this time instead of waiting 'til the end. I wanted to make sure that we started the argument that these players were retirees. Even Gene Upshaw, former president, claimed historically that the retirees were not bargained for during the collective bargaining process. We then added our argument that at the time we filed, there was no union, and the players were on strike, and other times when they played in the league, there was no collective bargaining agreement. Therefore, the NFL could not argue that the collective bargaining agreement required review since none existed at the time.

I then went over the other arguments that encompassed this case being brought as a state law violation by the National Football League. I tackled the issue that the NFL was a monopoly hiding the true effects of multiple concussions to scientists, doctors, and even parents. I covered the fact that the NFL committed fraud by lying to the players that they were not injured after they suffered a concussion or loss of consciousness. Then I presented the issue that the NFL licensed an unsafe helmet. This exact issue caused them to be liable and ultimately settle with Korey Stringer's estate.

I sent the response over to Bob Borrello for his edits, and then he shared it with Graham to add even more talent to this work product. I was exhausted after completing this project. It made me appreciate how difficult it is to win or even try to win a case of this magnitude.

By the beginning of January, we received more deadlines for the NFL's reply and our sur-reply brief. It was looking like we could have a decision by the end of the month on whether this case would survive to the next step which would be discovery. The discovery process would involve the review of all of the NFL internal documents as well as taking the depositions under oath of the doctors and executives from the NFL to determine what the league knew and for how long it failed to disclose this critical information about repetitive head trauma and brain injuries to the players.

In the interim, other lawyers were filing cases daily all around the country. The NFL got to the point where they could not keep up with these cases. Most of the lawsuits were now being filed in federal court. Therefore, the NFL saw it as an opportunity to seek the consolidation of the cases for pre-trial matters. Multi-district litigation, or MDL, is a consolidated approach to handle similar types of cases in front of one experienced judge tasked to handle all of the pre-trial matters. To obtain an MDL, there must be commonality of facts and law to the cases. MDLs also provide for consistency in rulings. All of these requirements were met because all the cases were the same since the lawyers had copied my template for their cases.

Therefore, the NFL asked whether we wanted to have our case stayed pending the decision and hearing of the MDL panel scheduled for late January. We ignored them as we felt good. Then the magnitude of the decision hit us as to whether the entire case could be dismissed. Was there a better location to get a ruling we were looking for? We, through the strong recommendation and assurances of Tom Girardi, ultimately agreed to stay Judge Real's determination of this historic decision. This would become a fatal decision in the quest for justice.

CHAPTER 32

Joining Together in Miami

We received an order from the judicial panel on multi-district litigation that an argument in regards to the NFL concussion cases would take place in Miami, Florida. It was scheduled to occur in late January 2012. By that time, there were about twenty lawsuits that involved well over a thousand former players.

The panel of federal judges asked for briefing as to whether anyone was opposed to the litigation being joined in one court. It was unanimous that all of the lawyers who represented players agreed that one courtroom was the preferred method to handle this case. The panel suggested as much during their questioning of the lawyers. However, the question of great importance was which federal courthouse should this case be transferred. Typically, this decision is largely based on two factors. The first factor is where the case was first filed. The second factor is whether that judge has experience or is capable of handling other MDLs.

It was clear that California was not the favored option by many lawyers. Since the first three cases of this litigation were filed and transferred to Judge Real, it was obvious that the next location of filing was Philadelphia. We all were unfamiliar with Philadelphia except for the fact that jury verdicts were typically favorable for plaintiffs.

In late January, at the MDL hearing, it allowed for the opportunity for all the lawyers to meet and jointly agree to work together for the best interests of the retired players. The meeting was hosted at the law firm of the Florida lawyers who entered the litigation around September. This firm of Podhurst Orseck was heavily involved in aviation cases and many class actions. They seemed to have a dozen attorneys working on the NFL case like it was a billable hour case. It left me curious why so many lawyers were thrown into a case with no certainty of any recovery.

It was quite interesting that most of the lawyers pretended like they had no idea who I was. Maybe they did not know of me and my relationship with Dr. Omalu. I was floored that they were talking about strategy of experts and they never once mentioned his name. I was confused. How could you possibly talk about medicine and factual discovery without having Dr. Omalu involved as your key witness?

After talking about witnesses and discovery of the NFL's knowledge of the brain injury crisis, Tom Girardi raised the issue of suing Riddell. Sol Weiss, a Philadelphia lawyer, quickly spit back that the key medical experts were conflicted as they already worked for Riddell. They said his name was Grant Iverson. I never heard of the guy.

As background, Sol Weiss was a partner with a Philadelphia firm on Anapol Schwartz. They were a plaintiff firm known for their extensive work in class actions involving pharmaceuticals, defective hips, and other related mass torts. Before I was ever born, Sol was a practicing lawyer. His website lists him as a class-action lawyer and lecturer on class actions. His website claims that he is a trial lawyer and it lists notable settlements. People who are trial lawyers inevitably try individual cases on behalf of their clients and ultimately have favorable results.

The next person that spoke about the case was an attorney from New York named Chris Seeger. Chris was a named partner of Seeger Weiss. He was not any relation to the Philadelphia lawyer. Chris was a much younger and polite lawyer. He never tried to show that he was smarter than the next lawyer. His actions told the story that he appeared to conduct himself in a polished and professional manner. Chris was also a class action lawyer and also helped injured people and was involved in handling asbestos cases for injured victims suffering from mesothelioma.

When there was finally an opportunity to speak after all the Philadelphia lawyers were trying to show how they were smarter than each other, Chris spoke about his relationship with Brad Karp. Mr. Karp was litigation counsel for the NFL. Chris announced that he had known Karp for a long time. He explained that he had been in negotiations with the NFL during the lockout. His goal was to provide a benefit to the players. He said that he exchanged his ideas of what the benefit for the NFL players who suffered brain injury would look like. Chris explained that when I filed the initial case, their conversations ended abruptly, and the NFL took what they were working on and created a new benefit and coined it the neurocognitive impairment benefit. He explained that the NFL's idea of this injury was that it was worth tens of millions of dollars in total to the retired players.

Chris seemed generally upset that the NFL gave him the stiff arm. Realistically, I could not imagine that he thought he should have been compensated for a benefit that was not in the best interests of all the players, and it also would give away their legal rights. This benefit was only created for players under the age of fifty-five years old. It also only applied to guys who played at least one year after 1994. At most, a player could receive $36,000 per year for this benefit.

Chris Seeger's emotions when telling this story was a mixed bag. I think he felt that I and these other lawyers who joined the fray hurt his chances of having a payday for this benefit. I think he was also sincere in stating that he had conversations with the NFL that showed that they were very concerned about this brain damage problem that they created.

Regardless, we left the meetings in Miami with Tom Girardi explaining that he went to all the lawyers present and told them that they all needed to work together. He said that he would agree to Philadelphia if they promised not to screw him. He seemed to get the assurances from them that made him satisfied. It made me satisfied as well.

During the actual argument in front of the judicial panel, they raised the issue of considering running our cases separately as California seemed to be the only location where Riddell was sued. In essence, they could run two pre-trial courthouses for the brain injury cases. One in California and one that housed everyone somewhere else.

During this time frame, everyone kept filing lawsuits and poaching our clients. If they were not filed, they were telling guys that they should file with them as it would preserve their legal rights. I decided that we had a number of new guys that we signed up by now. I decided that we should file them of record so that lawyers would stop stealing my clients. I also decided that we should file these claims in Philadelphia. I filed three cases comprising about 200 former players just days before the hearing in Miami.

As suspected, the judicial panel in Miami made that suggestion that I feared. They wanted to know why the California cases that included Riddell should not just stay in California since that was the only location where Riddell was facing lawsuits. I quickly ran up to Tom Girardi and whispered in his ear that we filed those cases in Philadelphia and it was no longer true that the only location where Riddell was sued was in California. He relayed this message to the judicial panel.

We left Miami feeling that the meeting was fair. Not surprisingly, it was going to be a little bit of a power struggle to determine who was going to be the leader of the group. However, it was clear that Girardi was the biggest lawyer in the group and the rest of the lawyers looked up to him.

I felt fine walking out of there. I did not think anyone would try to step on and over Tom Girardi. We also left the conference with the understanding that the lawyers would not talk to the press. They said that they would work on locating a public relations firm to help with these requests.

This agreement did not make it twenty-four hours. I received a call from a reporter asking questions about the litigation. I passed the inquiry on to the lawyer, who said he would arrange for the public relations group to help all of us. Lo and behold, there were quotes in the next morning's newspaper from this lawyer. Second, one of the Miami lawyers from Podhurst was on one of the ESPN shows talking about the lawsuit leading up to the Super Bowl. If that was not enough, another Philadelphia lawyer named Gene Locks advertised on his website that he was available for interviews at or during the Super Bowl. Gene Locks had a reputation for trying to get involved in any type of case from class actions to agent orange to personal injury matters. He had a reputation for doing things his way without any concern for his fellow lawyers. This was done with every communication that was sent en masse to players.

In the coming weeks, we received an order from the judicial panel consolidating all of the NFL concussions cases, including ours against Riddell, in federal court in Philadelphia. Since I was not licensed in that federal court, I asked one of my partners to take me to Philadelphia to be officially sworn in to their bar. We made that one-day trip by air the very next week in less than five hours. I was officially ready for the long litigation battle in Philadelphia.

CHAPTER 33

I Should Have
Gone to Harvard

Once the cases were consolidated in Philadelphia, we received a notification that Sol Weiss and his law firm were holding a meet and greet in Philadelphia that would discuss the law and medicine on day one, and on day two, all lawyers would discuss legal strategy.

When they were compiling the conference agenda, Tom Girardi insisted that he would fly in his neurological expert to discuss brain injuries. He explained that this expert was used in the Erin Brockovich cases. The folks at Sol Weiss's firm were not receptive to this suggestion. It was their meeting, and they did not want anyone to interfere with their agenda. Ultimately, they gave in to Tom and said they would fit in his expert at the end of their presentation.

Curiously, when I received the schedule of events, I was stunned to see that Dr. Omalu was not listed as a presenter. In fact, there was no neuro-pathologist to discuss chronic traumatic encephalopathy, a disease that could only be diagnosed by a neuro-pathologist upon death. I reached out to the lawyers at Sol Weiss's firm and asked if they thought this was a meeting that Dr. Omalu should be present. I did not receive any response.

The meeting was held at the law offices of Anapol Schwartz. It was a nice-sized conference room that could hold thirty or so people that had an adjoining side room that was typically used as an area to grab lunch. One of my partners, David Rodes, made the five-hour drive with me. We managed to make it to the meeting twenty minutes late and got a remaining seat in the adjoining room.

I walked into the first presentation being put on by Dr. Robert Cantu. Dr. Cantu is one of the leading experts on concussions and one of the neurosurgeons working with Dr. Omalu early during his findings of CTE. However, he had since left to form Boston University's Sports Legacy Institute with Chris Nowinski. Dr. Cantu's group had recently received a one-million-dollar grant from the NFL for their efforts in studying CTE. In turn, their group gave Commissioner Roger Goodell an award as the man of the year.

Dr. Cantu was obviously being compensated for his time to discuss brain injuries at this meeting by Sol's law firm. At one point, Dr. Cantu was a member of the NFL's Mild Traumatic Brain Injury Committee; at other times, he was a proponent supporting Dr. Omalu's findings of CTE, and then today, he had accepted an award from the NFL to research this issue. It made for a confusing situation, which I hoped he and Sol Weiss had cleared prior to attending.

Dr. Cantu continued to remain in the conference room as the other presenters discussed their issues with medicine. There were discussions on the evolution of concussion injuries. There were discussions by physicians on concussive and sub-concussive injury. Doctors spoke about neurology and treatment for their injuries. There was also a panel on other tests and scans that could be used to determine the extent of damage in the brain.

The other expert that Sol Weiss insisted on was Dr. Grant Iverson, who was working for Riddell. He was there to discuss the epidemiology and behavior patterns associated with the former NFL players. I too hoped he had cleared his conflicts prior to sitting in a room where my team was actively suing Riddell.

It took one of the lawyers in the audience to finally mention, after we had a moment to discuss the morning's events upon return from a lunch break, that there may have been a conflict of interest with Dr. Cantu being present. Not only was there a concern that Dr. Cantu had conflicts, but his presence may have just tainted the entire panel of potential experts. My first thought was thank goodness that Dr. Omalu was not present. My second thought was what about Grant Iverson. How was his presence not a conflict as well, especially if he worked for Riddell? I could not believe that these issues were never discussed with these experts. I was sure that the NFL would find out about this mess that was created by the experts and Sol Weiss's law firm. Of course, they did, and ultimately, they sent a stern letter about Dr. Cantu's presence at this meeting to Sol Weiss's law firm.

After the adventures of the morning were over, the afternoon consisted of legal experts in the area of class actions and preemption matters. There were three brilliant legal minds paid to educate us on the law. One was from the University of Pennsylvania, one from Yale, and then a Harvard guy.

I was not sure why there was an expert on class actions present for the legal panel. He was set to start off the afternoon session. I was curious if he would actually say that there was legal support to argue that this case could prevail as a class action. As suspected, he did not. Rather, for at least thirty minutes, he went over case by case by case as to why a brain injury class action against the NFL would never have any traction as a class action. He went over prior cases handled by the judge appointed to oversee the NFL litigation. Her name was Judge Anita Brody. He explained that Judge Brody was the most liberal of authorities in finding class actions. However, this case would never pass the smell test even with her.

After his presentation was over, I was laughing to myself inside. How could these lawyers want to file class actions after they were just embarrassed and told there was no legal support? I figured that was the end of the class-action discussion for the NFL concussion litigation.

The next person to speak was about the preemption argument. Everyone in the room was eager to hear what he had to say about the preemption issue. After all, he had argued other cases involving preemption in front of the United States Supreme Court on many occasions. He knew every case on point, and he knew the distinguishing factors that the court always hung their hats on when deciding the merits of each individual case. He explained that it was an issue that the Supreme Court of the United States had taken great interest in recent times.

He explained that the court could find labor preemption as to the general negligence claim. He said that we ought to spend more time developing the fraud claim. That advice cost $1,000 per hour. And to think that I spent the last five-plus years making no money to come up with the same information.

We took a mid-afternoon break for some snacks and refreshments. I figured that I would corner this expert and ask him some questions to see how much he really knew about this case in particular. He went straight for a cup of coffee, and I said thanks for sharing that information. I had a question for him regarding this case. I asked him if he was aware that the NFL players who played in the late 1980s into the early 1990s played without a collective bargaining agreement in place. I think he thought I was making this up. I asked him what bearing that would have on the NFL's preemption argument if there was no collective bargaining agreement, and then, based on what he told us this morning, the NFL would not be able to make the preemption argument in those cases. Then I asked him what he thought about the timing of our filing the first two lawsuits when there was no collective bargaining agreement.

He agreed with my analysis based on what he stated. He said that he really needed to give this issue more thought. He probably was thinking to himself, *Who is this young guy trying to tell me about preemption?* I think he probably was more concerned about getting some caffeine in his system as opposed to thinking that I captured the ultimate gotcha argument to the NFL's claim of labor preemption.

By the end of the day, I re-raised the issue briefly in the session with all lawyers present. It seemed to gather little to no interest. I think it was because no one ever thought of the issue or was even aware that this was an issue. We were on to a unique circumstance of winning a preemption issue when there was a strike. The lack of collective bargaining agreement would raise its head in the not-so-distant future as the key issue in the case.

CHAPTER 34

The Politics of Multidistrict Litigation (MDL)

The next day of the meet-and-greet at Sol Weiss's offices in Philadelphia was geared toward the strategy of handling the lawsuit. The evening prior was a dinner at Smith & Wollensky steakhouse, and then those of us who did not have an ax to grind grabbed some drinks at the hotel bar. I had an opportunity to get to know some really nice young lawyers at the Podhurst firm and, of course, the Atlanta lawyers.

Leading up to the conference, there were a number of groups that were sending e-mails with proposed case management plans and memorandum on various legal issues. The case management plan was a game plan for the pre-trial deadlines of the case.

There were also a number of e-mails going around that concerned the management structure of the case. The plan was to create an Executive Committee and a steering committee. The Executive Committee was a team of six law firms to oversee and lead the entire litigation. The steering committee was a committee of six other law firms that would serve the Executive Committee with providing the boots on the ground labor. The steering committee would lead the sub-committees of the litigation including the discovery, medicine, and the preemption committee by example.

The tension of this issue could be felt through the e-mails that were being exchanged. Sol's office said that there was an agreement of the lawyers who would sit on the Executive Committee. What agreement was that? How is it that was decided when there was no vote? There would be a handful of others that could serve on the steering committee if they could show past experience. Past experience in what? No one ever sued the NFL. They didn't understand the science or legal issues as was shown just earlier in the day.

By that evening's dinner, there were others that were sending e-mail messages expressing their dissatisfaction with the dictator system that did not include their names on either of these committees. Some did not understand how they could not serve on the steering committee when they were an earlier group of lawyers to file a case of their own. Others expressed great dissatisfaction in not being listed despite the fact that they served on just about every major class action steering committee.

I didn't understand the implications of serving on these committees. I figured that we would have a short stay in front of this court. Judge Brody would rule on preemption and then she would lose the authority to handle the case. It would have to be sent back to state court since she did not have federal jurisdiction at that point.

The class action lawyers who had intervened and taken the NFL case out of my control started to discuss time keeping and common benefit funds. I had no idea what they were talking about. I asked David Rodes about this issue. He explained that they do this in the event of a settlement. This way, they could seek funds separate from the client's awarded money. I asked David whether we should keep our time or if it would affect our ability to be paid our contingent fees. He responded that maybe I ought to generally keep track of my time. However, not to worry, it would not impact our contingent fees.

The leaders explained during the meeting that time sheets would be turned into one scorekeeper. They explained that common benefit time would start this month. They would not allow for time spent prior to February of 2012. Later, I learned that decision was the ultimate slap in the face of my efforts and the thousands of hours I put to get this case off the ground.

They explained that common benefit time was time spent for the good of all the players. You could not count any of your time speaking or working on behalf of your individual clients. They explained that assignments would be managed and controlled by the Executive Committee and that they would need to approve everyone's time sheets.

I gave them the benefit of the doubt. In large part, everyone was nice and welcoming at this two day meeting. It seemed like they really meant to work together as it would be a supreme task to take down the NFL in this case. They all gave the appearance that it would be an all-hands-on-deck approach to handling this case. The more hands, the better off we were to handle all the assignments that needed to be completed.

We also discussed a case management plan at this meeting. It seemed like lawyers were going to trip over each other volunteering to create a plan for pre-trial deadlines. I really did not understand the point of volunteering since every federal judge has their own discovery plan and they just plug in dates for each milestone.

The next part of the meeting moved into some discussion about filing class actions. They were all discussing a strategy on how and what state to properly file the class action. I could not believe they were not embarrassed to discuss class actions after that professor who spoke yesterday.

The meeting also addressed the next steps of preparing one master complaint and a short-form complaint that would provide individual information about our specific clients. I made sure I was on these committees that would be the first to meet.

Before leaving Philadelphia, I made sure that we filled the committees with names of lawyers from the three of our law firms. I think my name went into at least four of the ten committees. I was going to stay on top of every major activity in this case. I was going to remain positive that I would be playing a critical part on this case. Ultimately, the time would come when the case would require Dr. Omalu, and I would be the person to get him involved to help win the case.

CHAPTER 35

Working Together

The first committee to start working on the case was the legal committee. This committee was comprised of highly talented legal minds from Ivy League law schools who honed their careers behind a computer writing legal pleadings, briefs, and motions. This committee was tasked with taking all of our complaints and putting it into one complaint that would be the basis of the judge to rule on preemption.

There was no doubt in my mind that their writing talents would far surpass my legal writing ability. I was actually excited to see how well it would read. My biggest concern was assuring that the complaint contained all of the legal theories that I, along with Jack Tierney, had developed and became the basis of the NFL concussion lawsuits.

The draft of the complaint contained all of the background facts showing the NFL's coverup of the concussion issue that I revealed in the original complaint. It also tracked all of the findings of Dr. Omalu and the NFL's effort to have them retracted from the medical journals. It covered all of the scientific articles that I researched and found. It also covered the rule changes that were made by the NFL safety committee over the years.

The complaint spent numerous paragraphs discussing CTE. It specifically addressed the findings of CTE in the brains of Mike Webster, Andre Waters, Terry Long, and Justin Strzelczyk. They were the first four former players who Dr. Omalu found CTE in their brains after his autopsy evaluations. There was very little language about other brain injuries such as Alzheimer's disease, dementia or Parkinson's disease. Further, there was only one reference to ALS, or Lou Gehrig's disease in the entire one-hundred-plus-page complaint draft.

The first draft version of the complaint added some original material including some colorful highlights of the NFL's power and success. It talked specifically about their profiting from violence. It discussed their billion dollar television contracts.

The complaint alleged that the NFL became a monopoly. It talked about their power and authority over the science of concussion. It was right from Jack Tierney's theory that met the language of the Orlando *Brown* case head first. However, it did not create the cause of action as a count of the complaint. It alleged general negligence by the NFL.

The other thing that was curiously missing was the fact that the *Stringer* allegation that was successful against the NFL and NFL properties was missing. Again, the court in Stringer found that the NFL and NFL Properties failed in their duty to license safe equipment for Mr. Stringer. Where was the allegation that these two NFL entities failed to license a safe helmet for the players?

We had a conference call scheduled to discuss any thoughts about this complaint. I was prepared to raise those two important issues. I also needed to draft the language as it related to the Riddell allegations. They were not too happy that anything about Riddell was going in this master complaint. However, since one other law firm sued Riddell, they figured it was important enough to leave those allegations in the complaint.

I raised the two issues on the conference call. I was told by someone from Sol Weiss's team that they were not important. I said I do not see what the harm of including those allegations would be to the lawsuit. After all, they were successful claims that were litigated in the past against the NFL. They said that they were too far afloat from what they wanted to put in the complaint. I tried again. I said when we first filed this case, our decision was to throw everything at the league to try to prevail on this preemption argument. This is the reason we came up with the negligence monopolist theory and included the claim about licensing the unsafe helmet. Sol's partner was completely frustrated with me and my persistence on this call. His final response was, "If you want to make those claims, then I can put them in my short-form complaints for my individual clients." I was satisfied with that answer. However, I did not understand why they did not want these two additional claims in the master complaint.

There were no further telephone conference calls after this one. If there were others, I certainly was not invited to participate on those calls. There were occasional edits that would be exchanged through e-mails. None of the changes were of material significance. Ultimately, it seemed as though we had a satisfactory complaint.

The short-form complaint served to tell the story about each individual former player. It was created to provide background information on who the players were. The point of the short form complaint was to put the NFL on notice of the correct former player of the twenty thousand retired guys who were suing the NFL for brain injuries. It also served to allege what theories or claims the players were making against the league. It was different from the large complaint as it was only a few pages in length, but it provided the unique information about the player who was suing the NFL.

By now, there was also a class action master complaint. I still could not figure out why such a document was created after the devastating conversation one month prior at Sol Weiss' offices from the University of Pennsylvania law professor. Regardless, the short-form complaint allotted the plaintiffs with an opportunity to disclose whether they were seeking a class action, where their case was filed, and what theories of legal torts the NFL and/or Riddell committed against them.

I saw my influence on this case for the first time when I viewed the section in the short-form complaint. It said two very important things as it related to the negligence claims brought against the NFL. It stated negligence prior to 1969 and negligence between 1987 and 1993. I realized that I had personally discovered the critical issue that would help many players prevail in this lawsuit. These were the periods of time when the NFL operated without a collective bargaining agreement. It was the issue that I raised to that Harvard professor in the meeting in Philadelphia.

I know that the last versions of the complaint were blessed by the Harvard guy, and he must have told them to highlight those significant dates. It made me proud to realize that I actually knew more about this case than those lawyers who controlled the committees pretended to know.

My response to seeing this in writing was to tell the lawyer who sent it that he forgot about the period of three years in the late 1970s when they did not have a collective bargaining agreement as well.

All that needed done at this point was to file the master complaints, and then I would have to draft five-hundred-plus short-form complaints for all of my individual clients. I was certain that this project would make my assistant, Cindy DeUnger, and my secretary, Kim Siebert, very thrilled. I say that with great sarcasm. However, those two had become critical to me during this process that I would not have been able to pull off this case without their efforts.

Cindy had become my critical client support. She was constantly helping with client matters and questions that they continued to have. She soon learned what I had learned years prior. These guys would call and then, an hour, later call back with the same question. She was very polite and nice to them. During this time, she also helped fill the void for me of my lost mom. We have become very close friends, and I thank God she was there for me during these difficult years.

Kim Siebert has more years at our law firm than any other person or lawyer. She was a young when she started some thirty-plus years ago at what has become Goldberg, Persky & White. She was a top shelf secretary. She was a rarity that would actually fix grammatical errors in documents. She could locate documents from years ago in a matter of minutes. When you needed a contact phone number, she was able to find it in seconds.

Kim was able to create an organized system to track all of these clients information. She was able to create a process to e-mail the players to keep them informed. I was certain that our system she created was the most real-time means to advise our clients regularly.

They seemed satisfied with this approach as well as many of their friends would comment that their lawyers were not as on the ball as we were.

After the Complaint was filed, I shared it with the partners at my firm because I was proud of my efforts and vigilance to create this huge landmark lawsuit. When my partners realized as I did that our firm's name did not appear on the Complaint, they shared in my frustration and disappointment that all of my efforts to help former NFL players had been stripped away from me by cutthroat lawyers who didn't share in my passion to help the damaged athletes.

CHAPTER 36

The Fight for Clients

There was not a week that went by without me hearing about a client that was either hiring a new lawyer or signed with multiple lawyers. The players were inundated with messages claiming that one lawyer was better than another. Then the lawyers would tell each other that they should not be fighting over the clients. Then rinse and repeat the cycle of stealing each other's clients.

I am sure that this matter became the needed distraction that the NFL was hoping to achieve. The focus would deflect from them to the players and the lawyers fighting over the players.

It would cause some players to solicit others to join the lawsuits as some lawyers were making promises to them for delivering more clients. It would cause players to join this case despite the fact that they were not brain injured or even symptomatic.

One example of this behavior occurred when a backup quarterback by the name of Pat White joined the lawsuit. When he was offered a position to return to the NFL, he withdrew from the lawsuit. This created a lot of bad publicity for the players, resulting in losing some credibility for the impact of the lawsuit.

Lawyers were hitting up players associations. Lawyers were hitting up alumni conferences. Lawyers were soliciting workers compensation attorneys and player agents, asking to refer the lawyers these players. In turn, they would offer a large referral fee on the case in the event it was successful.

Lawyers would parade around the country, touting how many clients they signed up. They would argue that they had the most clients, so they were the biggest lawyer in the game. Others would promote the clients they represented as if the player were the game's best, therefore, he must have the best lawyer for this case.

Those who were harmed from all of this misinformation that was going around were the retired player community and particularly those who were brain injured. It is one thing to pry on a certain group of clients. However, these clients suffered brain dysfunctions that prohibited them to reason and function with executive and analytical skills to determine right from wrong.

One of the most egregious examples of this action involved a client of mine that was arrested for alcohol-related troubles. Some of his past troubles involved a vehicular homicide charge. However, his problems always stemmed around his brain issues that would cause him to black out or have seizures. One phone call I specifically recall was when this individual drove from his home in the great Northwest and ended up in Long Beach, California. He had no recollection of how he had gotten there. At any rate, he called and asked for help, asking me to provide his criminal defense attorney with information that his brain injuries from playing football were the reason he was having these driving problems. I sent him for an evaluation, which proved this medically. This medical report was used to get the former player out of his criminal conviction. Regardless of doing this task to save this player from jail time, I was eventually fired from my representation of him in the case for another lawyer who offered a cheaper deal. Years later, this player had CTE confirmed upon an autopsy of his brain after he passed away in his early fifties.

The endgame of all of these actions was to work out the representation of the player who signed with multiple attorneys by the attorneys. Ultimately, most of the time, we agreed to share fees equally upon recommendation from the Executive Committee. I just did not see how this decision to co-represent and share fees solved the problem of soliciting a represented party.

I was doing my best during this period of time to continue to promote our team that created and originated the lawsuit. It was our team who was the most competent and capable of taking this case all the way to verdict without the help of any other lawyers. I did that with my e-mail notifications to my clients. Some of those e-mails brought me to other players.

On two occasions, I ended up meeting the heads of players associations of retired players in the Arizona and New Orleans divisions. I was invited there to speak about the lawsuit and our team as to why the players who live in those communities should sign with my law firm. I learned pretty quickly that it was nothing more than a beauty contest. It was more about what you could give the players as opposed to why you could help the players the best. I refused to do any more of those engagements. I knew that grassroots word of mouth was the best way to gain the trust of these former professional athletes.

For all the bad that was going on with the lawyers and their fight over clients, there were still a number of good press issues. Players were speaking out about their brain damage. Hall-of-famers Tony Dorsett and Joe DeLamielleure had become the vocal voices of the retired players showing their unfair treatment as well as current disabilities. There were also guys like Dorsey Levins, Kyle Turley, and Kevin Turner, who suffered from ALS, that brought attention to this issue.

On top of that issue, there would be instances where other clients of mine would call me to help with their problems which would, in turn, pull me away from helping the case in general. In one instance, I received a call to help a client who was caught with his hunting guns in his car on a school campus when he went to pick up his child. He completely forgot that the guns were in his car after his hunting trip. He was charged with a felony. I had to help write letters and get him in the hands of a criminal attorney. Then I had to share his medical records that illustrated his dementia to help save him from jail time.

Another example was a client that was picked up by police with a charge of unlawful possession of a firearm inside a casino. Once again, his brain damage prohibited him from recalling that he had his gun on him and he forgot to bring along his gun permit. He was in a panic because he feared that he was going to face prison time and suffered from severe paranoia and claustrophobia. Ultimately, I was able to resolve this by having his firearm confiscated from his possession.

At the same time all of this was happening, there was an objective test that was developed by Dr. Omalu, Dr. Bailes, and Bob Fitzsimmons to test the brains of players to ascertain the level of a radioactive tracer in their brains that would bind the tau proteins so they could be observed in a PET scan. PET scan technology had been used in cancer patients to determine the growth of their tumors.

This test was offered through UCLA to some of the living players who I represented. ESPN ultimately released the findings in a story that brought them a Peabody nomination for the finding of CTE in the living players. Those who tested positive were my clients, Tony Dorsett, Joe DeLamielleure, Mark Duper and Leonard Marshall. This was a groundbreaking finding that quickly caused the NFL's "no CTE and no concussion" machine to quickly state that this was not medically proven quite yet. It reverted back almost ten years ago to when Dr. Omalu first founded CTE in Mike Webster. These same tactics were continuing.

There was one thing for certain. All scientists believed that technology was advancing enough that CTE would someday be able to be detected in the living.

Another positive change happened, but it took the ultimate price for someone. Junior Seau was one of the NFL's greatest linebackers of the 1990s and maybe the best player of that decade. He was elected to twelve pro-bowls over his twenty-year NFL career. Junior was a recognizable figure on and off the field for what he accomplished through his charity. However, in May of 2012, Junior no longer could handle the depression and cognitive battles he faced and was found dead with a self-inflicted gunshot wound to the chest. Every lawyer and every brain chaser went into action to attempt to lure the Seau family. Ultimately, the Seau's had his brain tested, confirming CTE, and hired a lawyer to join the litigation.

At this point forward, Junior Seau became the new face of CTE. He died in his early forties after just having completed his career. This disease clearly showed through Junior's suffering and death that it did not discriminate and was very deadly.

CHAPTER 37

Preparing the
Battle in Court

Around the time that everyone started filing the short-form complaints for their individual clients, the judge held a status conference. Judge Anita Brody was born in New York City in 1935. She obtained her law degree from Columbia University in 1958. In 1981, Judge Brody was appointed to the bench of the Commonwealth of Pennsylvania in Montgomery County Court of Common Pleas. Prior to this appointment, she had spent the majority of her career in private practice around the Philadelphia area. In 1991, she was appointed by President Bush to the federal judge position in the Eastern District of Pennsylvania.

Judge Brody held a status conference to schedule a timeline for the preliminary issues of the case. She adopted the recommendations for our meeting in Philadelphia. However, she added to that list her appointment of Chris Seeger and Sol Weiss as co-lead counsel. I was surprised that Tom Girardi was not appointed to one of these positions. I was confused how Tom was passed over. I was uncertain of the magnitude of these appointments, but I figured these lawyers could not take the case to trial without our help.

Judge Brody also set forth a scheduling order, putting together the timeframe as to the briefing of the motion to dismiss that the NFL was filing. It was expected to be due around the end of 2012 after many months of briefs, responses, replies and sur-reply briefs.

There was also a twenty-five-page limit to the written response to the NFL's motion to dismiss.

At the same time, Riddell asked to file an identical motion to dismiss. They also asked for an opportunity to file a motion to sever the claims from being tied to the claims brought against the NFL. Riddell asserted the same arguments they had previously, which I knew would not be successful in removing them from the litigation.

The Executive Committee decided to delegate the briefing on the response to the NFL's motion to dismiss to that Harvard preemption expert. It turns out that, despite the rumors, he was not even educated at Harvard. Rather, David Frederick was educated at the University of Pittsburgh. He then was a Rhodes Scholar in Oxford. Thereafter, he graduated from the University of Texas School of Law. He then went on to a clerk for U.S. Supreme Court Justice Byron White. He then spent a number of years as an assistant to the solicitor general to the United States. Currently, he spends his time in private practice representing companies, injured parties, and even the United States in cases in front of the Supreme Court of the United States and other appellate courts.

David Frederick and his law firm were hired to write the response that would decide the fate of the former players. By this point in time, there was a growing list of over four thousand former NFL players who had joined the lawsuit, with over forty law firms representing players.

I am not so sure that hiring Mr. Frederick was necessary as there were considerable talents to handle this task. However, in light of the overall lack of knowledge the player lawyers showed time after time, I was quite satisfied to see an expert on preemption involved in the key issue of the NFL concussion litigation.

In turn, Tom Girardi's office managed to be assigned the task of filing the responsive brief to the two Riddell motions. They immediately contacted us to prepare the responsive legal briefs. I was thrilled for the opportunity. However, this was old hat as far as I was concerned. I spent last Christmas preparing the same responses in Federal Court in the Central District of California. The work was done as far as I was concerned.

By this time, I was getting much needed help on the concussion case from my law firm of Goldberg, Persky & White. They would assign various people in and out of the case to help with a task or two that needed completed. On this project, I approached my firm's Executive Committee to advise them of this major assignment we were given on this case.

They asked that Jason Shipp work on the brief and that we seek counsel from Professor John Burkoff from the University of Pittsburgh Law School, who had advised our firm for many years. Jason Shipp was excited to step into this brief. He saw it as an opportunity to stand out among his legal department. He was a strong opinionated lawyer with supreme intellect. One time, he felt so strongly against this case in its early stages that he said I would never be able to pull it together because there was no legal claim. He was now a believer in this case and a big supporter of mine for pulling this together against all the odds.

Jason Shipp was thrilled to dive into dozens of cases. He sought out the help of another firm partner, Diana Jacobs, to read and distinguish every case cited in Riddell's brief. I, in turn, shared with him the brief that I prepared in California. I was no doubt confident that they would be able to put together an air tight brief.

I turned my attention to figuring out whether the preemption brief filed by the NFL would include the argument that the NFL owed a duty to license a safe helmet. I tried finding that out through Graham LippSmith, who was the partner looking over the case on Tom Girardi's behalf. He asked the co-lead counsel and received no response. I told him that we would need to brief that separately. He explained that doing so would piss off the others as we would stand out. I told him that our clients need the best shot possible to win this argument, and this was an important argument that had proven successful in the past. He agreed, so I started writing our response to file on behalf of our clients only.

I wrote that the NFL breached their duty to the plaintiffs by licensing the Riddell helmets to the players despite knowing or having reason to know that they were defectively designed and lacked an adequate warning. In turn, my clients developed latent brain injuries.

I wrote that this provision does not require looking into any collective bargaining agreement. The NFL argued that it required looking at the provision in the CBA on "Player Safety and Welfare." I argued that such provision is irrelevant to a merchandising company that was not part of the collective bargaining negotiations. Their decisions on the types of helmets to use and safety of them were well outside of any bargained for agreement between the players and the league management council. I argued that a decision by Judge Brody on this issue must be in tune with the Stringer Court, who found that the NFL Properties and NFL are not members of the player safety committee, and there would be no reason to interpret the CBA or adopt that committee's recommendation. The NFL and NFL Properties owed a duty separate from any CBA to ensure that the players had safe equipment. In total my responsive brief was three pages and was filed on Halloween in 2012.

The major NFL preemption brief was twenty-five pages in length and was a masterpiece of legal work, illustrating Mr. Fredrick's extensive experience on preemption issue. It was very well argued. The largest point of the brief was that the players who played during the periods when there was no collective bargaining agreement would not be subject to preemption. It made me proud that my discovery would be the most significant argument in a brief prepared by the expert on preemption issues in this country.

Meanwhile, Jason Shipp was doing an exceptional job illustrating that Riddell did not have the same argument as the NFL. They were not a party to the collective bargaining process. Rather, they were a third party that was a manufacturer of helmets. Not just any helmet, but they were also the official helmet and equipment manufacturer to NFL players. This exact claim was previously found to establish no preemption under the decision authored by the court in the *Stringer* case. This final version was finished by the end of October, with finishing touches put on it by Bob Borrello and Graham LippSmith. It was a solid work product.

Jason Shipp also was working on the response to Riddell's motion to sever. This was a motion that sought relief by Riddell from binding themselves to the NFL. They believed that, under the law, they had a right to have their claims heard in a separate lawsuit. However, we were able to piece together a litany of facts illustrating their tightly bonded relationship with the NFL. We were able to illustrate in the brief that Riddell was an integral part of the NFL's cover up on the concussion issue. They too, as well, were aware of the science of concussion but failed to put a concussion warning on their helmets when my clients played in the league.

Both of these responses were prepared to file with the others on October 31, the date when the court required them to be due. We sent it on to Graham to get it filed by the Executive Committee. The court system is an electronic filing system. It operates to save paper, make sure things are timely filed after the close of the courthouse, and it provides instant real-time notifications to all counsel of any filings on the docket.

I watched our brief that was filed in the case. Curiously, the only thing that had changed after it left my law firm's hands was that our names were no longer affixed to the response. I could not figure out why someone would delete our names. I couldn't imagine a publisher deleting the author's name on a book and putting his name on the work. Truly a selfish move by someone on the Executive Committee.

By the beginning of 2013, all of the motions, responses, replies, and sur-replies were complete. It was now in Judge Brody's hands to schedule an oral argument to hear the lawyers state their legal arguments in front of her.

CHAPTER 38

Getting Kicked to the Curb

The big date for oral argument was going to take place in April 2013. It was gathering media attention across the country, with print journalists and television cameras everywhere. It was going to be the super bowl matchup of the case.

The NFL hired Paul Clement to argue their preemption argument. Paul Clement served as the solicitor general to the United States by nomination of then President George W. Bush. His distinguished legal career consisted of graduating magna cum laude from Harvard Law School. He took on President Obama's Affordable Care Act in the court system, worked as a law professor at Georgetown Law School and, most importantly, argued over fifty times before the United States Supreme Court.

On behalf of all the players, David Frederick was set to argue why this matter was outside of any collective bargaining agreement and deserved to be heard in a court of law. The lawyers were all satisfied with this decision. It should not be about the attorneys representing the players. It should be a decision that was in the best interests of the clients. By far, David Frederick gave us the best opportunity to win.

It was so crowded that I could not find room in the main courtroom. I, however, was able to get a seat in the honorary courtroom that had a satellite feed of the live proceedings. There were cameras and people talking about the day everywhere. Some players even made the journey to watch the historic arguments on the nation's most talked about lawsuit ever.

Since the NFL filed the motion, Paul Clement argued first that because issues of health and safety were covered by collective bargaining agreements with the players' union, the matter should be subject to grievance procedures and arbitration. It did not belong in court. Specifically, the NFL's position was that Section 301 of the Labor Management Relations Act prevents lawsuits that would require a judge to interpret provisions of the collective bargaining agreement.

Paul Clement voiced, "Here, the subject of the dispute—player health and safety issues—is mentioned throughout the agreements."

David Frederick took Judge Brody's advice on that warm early April day in Philadelphia and removed his suit coat. He stood confident and countered that the NFL's claim was stratospheric and that Judge Brody does not even have to consider any CBA. He said the NFL was bound by common law to safeguard the players and that it instead misled them. "What the league is trying to do here is get immunity. That has nothing to do with the basic breach of duty that we're asserting here," argued Frederick.

David Frederick then raised those issues that I uncovered back in 2006 and into 2007—that the collective bargaining agreements did not address such issues as long-term effects of concussions. He said Section 301 of the Labor Management Relations Act does not apply. He stated that the agreements do not address the allegations of this concussion lawsuit, which stated that the league spread misinformation about concussions.

Judge Brody showed her neutrality during the confrontation, asking very pointed questions to each lawyer. Oftentimes, she even stopped them mid-sentence to raise important issues regarding the legal claims made by the players and defended by the National Football League.

Judge Brody pressed the NFL lawyer to show her where provisions of health and safety were all over the past CBAs. Paul Clement said provisions about health and safety were all over the past CBAs. Judge Brody quickly snapped back, "Tell me specifically. How am I supposed to know that it relates specifically?"

David Frederick faced the same difficult questions from Judge Brody, exploiting the weakness in just simply arguing the negligence claim. David Frederick cited a number of cases that supported the claim that there should not be preemption. Judge Brody was quick to point out that "there are a number of cases throughout the country that have gone the other way."

However, the true highlight of the argument for me was when Judge Brody quickly realized the hole in the NFL's argument. She asked Paul Clement, the NFL lawyer, how the NFL could argue that they were entitled to preemption during the periods of when there was no collective bargaining agreement. Clement acknowledged that that was a problem for the league.

The arguments for Riddell were next on the agenda to take place after lunch. Many of the seats were empty after the arguments with the NFL were completed. Tom Girardi had decided that the best approach for this argument was to use a lawyer who had handled arguments in many of his past cases. Martin Buchanan is an appellate lawyer who has handled hundreds of legal appeals. He, as well, graduated from Harvard Law School, graduating magna cum laude. He had successfully argued in front of the United States Supreme Court.

Judge Brody quickly asked Martin Buchanan and the Riddell lawyer about the claims brought against Riddell. She asked whether they were the same arguments that were raised in the past couple of hours involving the NFL. Martin Buchanan quickly pointed out that they were not even close to the same types of arguments. Riddell was not a party to the collective bargaining process. There was not a single duty that they can point to that was negotiated as to player safety, concussions, or wearing equipment that was specifically drafted in the NFL's CBA with Riddell in mind. Buchanan explained that this identical issue was litigated in the *Stringer* case, and the court swiftly denied their preemption claim.

The argument was short and concise. He was on top of every issue in the case. You could tell that arguing legal issues was his comfort zone. It was as if there was no argument that Riddell raised had any effect on his calm and collected demeanor. He responded swiftly with short focused points that he raised convincingly before Judge Brody.

I left Philadelphia feeling pretty good about our case. I felt that Riddell had no argument and that was clearly relayed to Judge Brody. I felt that we outperformed the NFL on the preemption argument. I, along with the many lawyers I spoke with, felt positive about prevailing on parts of that claim. Even if we survived on one of our arguments, all of the lawyers would finally have the opportunity to conduct discovery against the NFL. This was the league's biggest fear as it meant that years of information which the NFL had hidden and suppressed would finally be brought to the attention of the lawyers involved in this case, current and former NFL players, and public at large.

CHAPTER 39

Preparing for the Next Step

After the argument, I felt like the race to prepare my clients' cases for the discovery process was going to start. At that point in time, there was a change in my team. Jack Tierney had finally retired around February 2013, three years after his original retirement party. By the spring time, another experienced attorney offered his assistance to the case. Mike Elmer was a senior lawyer who had come back to Goldberg, Persky & White more than twenty years after he had left to take on a different practice venture. Mike was very detail oriented. He carried around three or four different colored pens and a school notebook, not a legal pad, to keep track of each individual project which he was working.

Mike had just finished working on a case concerning a toxic exposure to a small town. He was able to uncover the secret smoking gun documents in that case. After that case wrapped up, he came to me and volunteered to help on the NFL case. He saw it as an opportunity to help guys in a sport which he followed their careers. Also, Mike bled civil justice. He saw the NFL as an evil empire that was the epitome of corporate indifference to human health, and we were fighting with God, truth, and justice on our side.

I welcomed Mike's assistance. As much as he was different from Jack, he had many of the same qualities in persistence to the point of overworking each and every detail of a case. I immediately tasked

Mike to help organize our client files and figure out where they all stood medically with their brain injuries.

In the meantime, all attorneys had received a request from the Executive Committee of the NFL concussion case to complete a questionnaire for every individual client. The questionnaire consisted of over thirty different brain-related conditions and problems. The objective was to have your client report whether he had been diagnosed or experienced any of these problems. In other words, we were asking brain-injured people to actually understand and complete a detailed document describing their brain injuries. Not a realistic task that any neurologist would expect from their patients.

Regardless, I sent out the questionnaire in a green form and reminded my clients constantly to complete it. I ended up getting a return of one hundred to two hundred forms out of the five-hundred-plus clients that I represented. Not surprisingly, the guys who completed the forms were generally mildly symptomatic. The phrase mild associated with a brain injury is a misnomer. Over the years, I have made a point discussing brain injuries as a serious problem that a Band-Aid, cast, or stitches could not fix. The phrase mild should be saved for food ingredients and spices.

I shared the responses from my clients with the NFL Executive Committee, who used it to gain an idea of the types of clients involved in the litigation and the extent of their brain damage. I was hopeful that it would not be used as a basis of any statistical information for the case.

The Executive Committee of the concussion case also asked to send a letter to the commissioner of the NFL on behalf of the retired players. They shared a draft of the letter with all persons who represented NFL Hall-of-Famers. The letter related that the league failed in its role to take care of its own. The Hall-of-Famers expressed their desire to see those who suffer from debilitating brain injuries to get the help that they need immediately. It also reminded the league of their distinction as the best players to ever play the game and the need for the league to act at their request. As expected, there was nothing that came of this letter.

One of the things that I experienced weekly was numerous requests from scientists and physicians requesting to utilize their services as experts in the case. All of a sudden, everyone was purporting to be an expert in football brain injuries. Most of the people talked about outrageous products that they offered to test the players. Others claimed that they had researched these issues for years but never published in peer literature their findings. It became apparent that this was the new sexy issue to attempt to make a profit. Unfortunately, it was at the hands of brain-damaged football heroes of the past. I could imagine how Dr. Omalu felt to see these folks come out of nowhere to purport to have the book on brain injuries. I am sure he felt just like me when all the lawyers came into this lawsuit after the risk I took to file it.

I knew that my main task was to figure out how to prove the cases for my clients individually. In order to do that, I had to show that playing football in the NFL was causative of their injuries. One of the questions that had always been raised in this case was how can you show that their brain injury did not start in pee wees, high school, or possibly playing college football.

To understand this issue, it is important to combine the law and science. Under the law, most courts require proof of causation of an injury and require that a person show that the defendant was a substantial contributing factor in bringing about the injury. As the lawyers representing former players, our burden would be to show that playing football was a factual cause of the player's injury. It need not be the only cause. There could be many causes. However, playing in the NFL must have been a substantial cause. It could not be a remote or fanciful cause.

I spent a considerable about of time discussing this issue with many experts. However, there was one expert that had illustrated time and time again that the players' injuries in the NFL were substantial contributing causes. Dr. Bennet Omalu likened the cause of CTE in the football players to exposures that workers suffered to asbestos.

In the asbestos world, experts have testified for decades that exposures are total and cumulative in nature—that there is not one exposure that is less important. Rather they are treated with equal condemnation. It's the idea of three factories spreading toxic chemicals in the water that killed the fish. Each of the factories alone could have killed the fish; however, in combination, they were all substantial reasons that the fish died.

Bennet explains that CTE is a cumulative disease that is caused from numerous hits. It is not a concussion disease. Unfortunately, this very fact is the issue that the football world does not want us to know. They want everyone to believe that CTE is a concussion disease. They want everyone to believe that this case is about a concussion or concussions that may cause a later life problem.

To the contrary, this lawsuit is specifically about multiple brain traumas that are concussive and sub-concussive in nature. It is the repeated and continuous blows to the heads that are causative.

When you think about a football career, it typically starts at a younger age where the kids play a few practices a week and possibly a handful of games. When they make the high-school level, it is roughly ten games per year with more practices on the schedule. Most kids do not get much playing time until their junior or senior seasons. While in college, you have eleven or twelve games and a spring practice and late summer training camp and regular practices. Again, the typical player is not getting on the field his first two seasons.

When you make it to the NFL, it becomes your job. It is a full-time career. There is football eight to nine months out of the year. There are mini-camps, training camps, four pre-season games, daily practices, and at least sixteen regular season games if your team does not make the playoffs.

For years, NFL teams practiced two times per day in training camps in full pads. Until recently, teams practiced daily during the season in full pads. One of my clients, Alexander "Woody" Thompson, described his practices with the Atlanta Falcons of the late 1970s. The defensive coordinator at the time was Jerry Glanville. He had some of the best defenses and physical players of that time period. His practices were so physical that, by game day on Sunday, the players were too beat up to actually go out and play to win.

Another player from the 1990s retired after twelve successful NFL seasons as a tight end. He once told me that he should have played fifteen or sixteen seasons. I looked at him confused. He said practices were so physical back then. You never practiced without full pads. Today's players rarely hit in practice let alone wear their full pads. It makes sense.

Proving the player's injury was caused from the NFL is not so difficult under the legal and scientific burden of proof. Unless the player only was in the league for a season or two, the ability to prove their injury was total and cumulative is rather basic science.

By way of example to show the amount of times a former player would strike his head, one of the former player's doctor calculated that over his 10+ year NFL career, this player struck their head at least 225,000 times. This calculation is based on the number of practices and games an NFL player will participate in over the length of their career.

Based on all of this, it was apparent that I needed to contract with Dr. Bennet Omalu to exclusively agree to testify as the expert on CTE on behalf of my clients. This was a distinct advantage that only my clients had over the rest of the field of lawyers. I was therefore ready for the next step. All we needed was to get the order from the Court dismissing the NFL's preemption argument, which was now expected to be a specific date in July 2013.

It seemed as though everything was lining up in our favor. The NFL recently was given a black eye due to a scandal involving the New Orleans Saints. The New Orleans Saints were caught having a bounty program. It was a non-contractual incentive programs that involved injuring the opposing team's best players for additional bonus money.

This bounty program was uncovered by Sean Pamphilon a successful filmmaker who was working on a documentary piece involving a former Saint. Sean had captured film footage and audio of Greg Williams, a defensive coach of the New Orleans Saints, encouraging the defensive players to injure another player, and he would pay the first bounty award.

The second issue during this period of time for the NFL was bigger than a black eye and hurt brain. It involved a player who came into the league with known baggage. Aaron Hernandez was drafted by the New England Patriots in 2010 despite having a known rebellious nature and having admittedly failed multiple drug tests in college. In 2013, Aaron Hernandez was arrested and charged with the murder of his friend, Odin Lloyd. The police later uncovered footage from Hernandez's home showing security camera footage that appeared to show him holding a handgun shortly after the time of the murder at 3:30 a.m. Later, authorities uncovered ammunition and clothing possibly linked to the murder of Mr. Lloyd at an apartment owned by Hernandez. Aaron Hernandez was instantly cut and released from his $19 million remaining contact with the Patriots. A photo of Hernandez in the NFL Hall of Fame in Canton, Ohio, had to be removed after visitor complaints. Hernandez was indicted by a grand jury for the murder of Mr. Lloyd. He faces a criminal trial with first-degree murder charges. Was he yet another example of a brain-injured football player who had uncontrollable impulses? Years later, after he committed suicide in prison, his brain tested positive for the most severe CTE ever found in an individual of his age.

These issues were ultimately very damaging moments for the league, which was caught in a scandal involving hurting players and people when we were pursuing a lawsuit that was all about the league not protecting the player's brains. It was even more evidence to support the case—a case that I suspected would soon enter the discovery phase.

CHAPTER 40

The First Settlement

The argument on the NFL and Riddell's preemption matter was in early April of 2013. By mid-June, there were a number of reporters and people that were calling the court to inquire when Judge Brody's decision would be made. In June, she sent out an order that her decision would be issued in mid-July. There was no need for anyone to keep contacting her chambers.

However, the next play in the case was an "end around." Judge Brody, as quickly as she had stated when her order would come out, ordered the parties to mediation. Mediation is a court's attempt to appoint a neutral person to attempt to resolve the lawsuit or narrow the issues in the case. In this instance, Judge Brody appointed Layn Phillips.

The Honorable Layn Phillips was a former federal judge in Oklahoma. He later went into private practice in Newport Beach, California. He has served for many years as a mediator and helped settle thousands of complex civil cases.

I had mixed feelings about the mediation. I was concerned who would be involved in the process. I expected that the Executive Committee would make sure Tom Girardi was present. However, I was concerned how they valued this case this early in the process or even if it was possible to make such predictions regarding the amount of the settlement this early in the litigation. It was way too early to determine its value since the major issue of the case had not been decided. On the other hand, I was very excited about the mediation.

I was proud. I had taken this matter from nothing. I couldn't even get a moment of anyone's time to discuss this case. It was now potentially going to settle and vindicate Dr. Omalu's name and offer financial help to these former players and their families.

During those months, I received various requests from Tom Girardi asking for specific documents. He wanted to know revenue breakdown. I was able to gather that information. He wanted to know the types of benefits the players received. I was able to track that down. He wanted to know specific amounts of benefits that the players received monthly. Again, these tidbits of information, as well as a number of other documents he requested, were quickly gathered and provided to Tom. It led me to believe that our clients would be protected and the end result would be a fair deal if Tom was involved.

By August, I had not heard much communication from Tom Girardi. I assumed that he had everything he needed and he would update us with a confidential conversation if there was sufficient progress in the negotiations with the NFL. This never happened.

On August 29, I was sitting in a meeting with a few of my partners. An e-mail came across my iPhone announcing the agreement to settle on the electronic docket. I could barely breathe. I was so excited to find out what it was. I asked Jason Shipp to print it off the docket. The court notification announced a $765 million dollar settlement with the NFL. I was confused. My original thought was there must be more to it. Maybe this was just the first payment.

I read more details from the order of court. The details illustrated that it included a fee of $112 million in common benefit fees to the attorneys. The number immediately grabbed my attention as being rather high. How could they pay the attorneys this number and then attorneys like me would be able to take their large contingent fees. Something was not adding up after my initial glance at this settlement.

Then, we received a short e-mail from the co-lead counsel announcing how great the settlement was for my clients. It had enough money to last sixty-five years. It would provide payments as much as $5 million to those most severely injured. My instincts and my skills with math made me raise my eyebrows over this announcement.

Something did not seem right. There was only one person to ask to figure this out. Immediately, I spoke with Herman and Bob who were very happy that they teamed up with me to take on this endeavor. However, we agreed that we needed to speak with Tom Girardi to get his interpretation on this settlement.

We tried non-stop to get a hold of him. However, it took until September 6, when he actually spoke with Herman over the phone. In the meantime, there were numerous rumblings of articles where the press was criticizing the terms of the settlement. Most of the criticism surrounded the fact that the number was curiously way too low given the value of the NFL, which is worth billions.

There were reports that only the most severely injured would get paid out of this deal. It would leave many of the players out in the cold. This issue gave me pause.

There were other reports that that the players sought over $2 billion from the NFL but settled for this figure. It appeared as though the settlement was yet another black eye for the lawyers selling the players short to only benefit themselves. It seemed like another slight in a long history of the players getting this poor treatment.

Finally, we heard from Tom Girardi. He was not the least bit pleased with the result. Many of the things he could not tell us about due to confidential reasons. The judge had signed an order stating that the mediations were to be kept confidential between the parties. However, we did learn that he was not part of the final negotiations. We also learned that the co-lead counsel was ready to throw in the claims against Riddell into this settlement and dismiss them from the lawsuit. This was truly unbelievable to even imagine how they could do such a thing when they did not even sue Riddell.

This confirmed my worst fears that the settlement was not fair for the players. It confirmed my fears that we once again would spend our time fighting with the lawyers who created this deal as opposed to representing our clients in court against the parties that caused their brain injuries.

More and more time passed, and there was no announcement of the official terms of the settlement. I never heard of such a thing. How can you create a settlement and not have the terms of the deal finalized? How were the terms of the settlement not publicly filed for everyone to review?

Players were very angered during this stage. They were talking and doing whatever it took to hire and fire lawyers left and right. I spent most of my time over the next few months reassuring them of confidence in our fight. I was explaining that I did not create the deal. I explained that we still can fight on, and I was glad that we had Riddell as a party to litigate against.

It took until early January 2014 before the terms of the deal were made public. An entire regular season in the NFL was played before the terms of the deal were shared with the players or their lawyers. I could not believe it. The deal consisted of over 100 pages of settlement documentation. After digesting it, I was completely disgusted with many provisions in the NFL settlement agreement. The thing that stood out the most to me was that this no longer was a CTE case. It was a case that simply provided a benefit to guys with severe neurological symptoms.

The settlement lawyers sought Judge Brody's preliminary approval of this class action proposed settlement. They filed papers insisting that the player's claims were similar enough and that they created a grid to compensate those who were injured.

Within one week of filing the motion, Judge Brody swiftly rejected the preliminary approval of the settlement. She wrote that she was concerned that there were insufficient funds to pay all of the injured players over the course of the next sixty-five years. She also had concerns about the releasing of lawsuits by the players against colleges and other leagues. These were a few of the concerns that she noticed when co-lead counsel filed this motion to get their money for the short amount of work they put into the case.

In the meantime, we received a notification from the lawyers who crafted this settlement to come to New York so they could discuss the benefits of this settlement with all lawyers who represent former players. By then, Tom Girardi and I had engaged in a public criticism of the settlement terms. I took my partner, Bruce Mattock, with me to the meeting. Also, Bob Borrello and Graham LippSmith came to join our coalition. We would certainly be coming to it as the unwelcomed outsiders.

The meeting gave me the feel of walking into a retail store with an overabundance of salespeople trying to make a commission. It moved quickly to a question-and-answer session to allow the lawyers to finally have answers to their burning questions concerning the settlement. There were a few softball questions. Then I stepped in and asked over 70 percent of the questions for the next two hours. I could tell they were clearly annoyed with every question that I asked that went to the heart of the weaknesses of this settlement.

I asked them why they used the families of Webster, Long, and Strzelczyk to just shun them from qualifying under the deal. Co-lead counsel stood at the front of the ballroom and just stared at me like I had three heads. They could not understand why I was asking them that question. I simply responded that they used these three guys as the backdrop of the CTE case and then negotiated away their claims. On top of that, I asked how they turned this case from a CTE case to a lawsuit about ALS and dementia. They responded to that question about whether I think that an ALS disease is the most serious neuro-logical condition. I responded that it was the most serious condition, but the last time I checked, there was only one reference in the entire complaint to ALS being linked to playing football. I again repeated how they could change this case from CTE to an ALS and dementia case. I did not receive a response.

I asked about the lack of behavioral symptoms as being part of the compensation plan. I asked how this settlement took care of for-mer players that had depression and were suicidal. They responded that the population at large has those problems. Someone else asked them if they were aware of tests that could diagnose CTE while play-ers were still living. They responded that those tests were not medi-cally accepted yet.

After the meeting ended, a couple of things were clear to me. First, I did not think the lawyers who negotiated the settlement understood CTE. Second, I felt that they were minions of the NFL's position. This became clear to me when I cornered both Sol Weiss and Chris Seeger separately to ask them what amount of the $112 million common benefit fund I earned for my efforts. Their unified separate responses were that I get nothing out of that work prior to February 2012. All the common benefit work started in February of 2012 when the NFL got these lawyers to control the case so they could walk away from this issue of CTE and football players once and for all time.

There were a few bright spots that happened at this meeting. I got a chance to meet some other lawyers who shared these same frustrations with this settlement and believed that the players deserved better. One was a guy that previously worked for one of the firms that was part of the Executive Committee. His name was Brad Sohn. He played college football with Chris Nowinski and shared the same passion for the players and the issues. Brad practices out of Miami.

Another strong advocate was a young lawyer who created a website to track the progress of this case. When he saw the actions of these bad lawyers, he jumped into the case, rounding up clients for his practice in Missouri. Paul Anderson quickly became an expert and advocate to keep the litigation going and not settle early.

Lastly, I had the opportunity to meet Tom Demetrio and Bill Gibbs. These guys are trial lawyers out of Chicago. They were very strong advocates for the case and challenged lead counsel every step of the way for selling the players short on this settlement.

With the settlement taken away, I was unsure where this was all going to end up. It felt once again that the bullseye was taken off of the NFL and placed on the lawyers fighting over each other.

CHAPTER 41

The Actual Settlement

The solution to the problem with the original proposed settlement was Judge Brody assigned a special master to review the settlement data and actuarial tables to determine if this settlement was sufficiently funded to pay the life of the claims. She also sent the parties back to mediation.

There was an enormous push back to co-lead counsel, Chris Seeger and Sol Weiss, to share the actuarial data with all of the lawyers. This data was pulled together by an expert to determine the amount of payouts over the life of the settlement fund. I was not so concerned with seeing the data. I was sure that it was flawed. It was believed that the data were from the forms that our individual clients filled out. Those same forms for which only one-third were returned to me by my clients. Those same forms that also asked brain-injured players to confirm their neurodegenerative problems. It also was rumored that the data took into account the fact that 15,000 of the players who never sued did not play more than two years. They would not have compensable claims.

Whether they were using these assumptions or other data such as statistics from workers compensation cases, claims made to Plan 88, or even NFL data collected on retired players, I felt highly confident that the values were grossly underestimated. The reason for that is that the typical retired player suffered brain damage. Most were not married. Most former players certainly were not trusting and skeptical of others purporting to offer assistance. So in total, they lacked advocates to assist them with their daily lives. Further, most retirees were unaware of their brain injuries due to their lack of health care coverage to pay for any doctors. Finally, even if they got past all of the above, then the retired brain-injured player had no one who was qualified to help them obtain Plan 88 benefits to help with their medical care. This was the benefit named after John Mackey that provided for medical care for dementia and other severe neurodegenerative diseases. This explains why there were less than 200 former players qualifying for this benefit.

My time on the first settlement had better uses. I was more curious in exploring what the settlement meant to my clients. I realized that most of the guys would not qualify. However, I believed that there were many guys who were walking around with early dementia or Parkinson's Disease and were simply unaware of it.

In order to determine this, players had to undergo the battery of tests that the settlement called for. It was a curious battery that consisted of neuropsychological testing and then an evaluation by a neurologist. The neuropsychological testing is more of a question and answer test that evaluates your cognitive loss in comparison to your pre-morbid level. In other words, it tests where you used to be when you were at your brain's prime level to where you are today after your cognitive loss.

The neuropsychology test determines losses in five cognitive domains including complex attention, executive functioning, learning and memory, language, and perceptual-spatial. The neurological test determines your cognition along with the player's functional loss. The neuropsychological test battery takes over five hours to complete. I liken it to an IQ test on steroids.

I rounded together my team of lawyers and employees willing to help evaluate our client's cognitive capabilities and functional impairment to determine whether they were a candidate for testing with experts. Mike, Cindy, Kim, Jason, Diana, and a law clerk or two helped on occasion, reviewing files and calling our clients. Mike was largely in charge of tracking down past medical records, especially for those rare clients who had prior diagnoses and treatment for their cognitive problems. He also had to find informants to confirm if those with cognitive impairment were no longer independent in their activities of daily living.

The evaluations revealed some very alarming details of the lives of these players. It was information that even went further and deeper than even I was aware involving the extent of their injuries. One guy who played thirteen years in the NFL was an example of alarming problems common to the former NFL player. The neurologist and the neuropsychologist found that he had short-term memory problems, confusion, frustration, planning deficit, problem solving deficit, dysnomia, slurred speech, reading comprehension deficit, articulation problems, slowed reaction time, temporal disorientation, distractibility, disorientation and confusion, weakness, balance problems, dizziness, slowed movement, problems with initiation, fatigue, numbness, headache, urinary incontinence, loss of bowel control, depression, anxiety, sleep onset problems, anger, loss of libido, loss of joy. and to top it off, he was diagnosed with Parkinson's Disease.

As suspected, there were more guys than I originally anticipated that showed signs of dementia, Alzheimer's disease, or Parkinson's disease. These guys just were never made aware of their link to football and these various neurological conditions. When they went to a doctor, no one was looking for these conditions because they were not over age sixty-five. Approximately 25 percent of my clients were found to have one of the qualifying diagnoses under the terms of the settlement. Over their lifetime, I think it would be safe to assume that figure should grow another 10 percent of my clients. Therefore, as suspected, my analysis of my sampling of 500 clients should yield a diagnosis of one of the neurological and cognitive problems related to football at a figure over one-third. That is the bad news for the players. If they played the game that long, close to half of them in my analysis would develop a chronic debilitating early neurocognitive condition associated with the older population, which the settlement was designed to compensate them.

Those others that did not develop symptoms may still have CTE upon their death. Studies have shown that nearly 99 percent of former NFL players had CTE in their brains. Alarmingly, many never had a concussion or any cognitive symptoms during their lifetime. Dr. Omalu truly should be proud of himself for uncovering this condition. However, it took a lawsuit to put these players into statistical figures of serious brain injuries.

When the settling lawyers were ultimately required to share their actuarial data regarding the settlement calculations, their data showed a 28 percent development rate in these conditions in the player population. Again, the problem of these statistics were that they were based on self-reporting of the players and they ignored the fact that these diagnoses tend to develop at a much earlier age in football players.

Alan Schwartz once reported and wrote that NFL players were five to nineteen times more likely to have a dementia-related diagnosis than the general population. This finding and filing in the court record corroborated what Alan Schwartz was the first to report on in the media.

My strategy of evaluating my clients proved to be the right maneuver while the lead counsel and the NFL were renegotiating the settlement. Turns out, we did not hear anything concerning the settlement or negotiations until June of 2014. During that entire period of time, they did not communicate with Tom Girardi despite the fact that he was on the Executive Committee of the case and was advising over a thousand former players on whether or not to accept the terms of the settlement.

In June, we learned that the deal was largely the same; however, the settlement of $765 million was now an uncapped fund. This meant that, hypothetically, the NFL could pay billions in claims. To protect that from happening, they added a more strenuous checks-and-balances system to review all claims seeking compensation. This meant that the NFL would be involved individually on whether any former player should or should not be paid. In other words, this was no longer a settlement offering a benefit to all former NFL players, but rather turned into a claims processing agreement similar to how the government compensates individuals who develop black lung disease.

They did not touch many of the provisions that mattered the most. They did not deal with the issue of CTE. If you died from

CTE from now into the future, then you did not get paid. The reasoning of co-lead counsel is that it would promote suicide of the players. I disagree with that assessment strongly. This case has always been about CTE. In order to deal with this public health crisis, there should be requirements to study football players and science and rule changes to better play that game to promote the players and their long-term health. It would also provide critical data to doctors, scientists, coaches, players, and parents to assess the rate of CTE in football players.

There were also no provisions for new testing platforms that could identify CTE in the future. The players were never considered to undergo the PET scans nor all these other new tests.

These changes, in large part, caused the settlement to become more of a deal than not a deal. The reasoning was that most courts have unanimously certified any settlements which had an uncapped payment plan. Since this was the case, I expected any appellate court to agree that this settlement was fair, reasonable, and adequate as it addressed the claims made by the players in the lawsuit.

I expected some pushback from the settlement from groups of lawyers. However, I made peace with settlements being hard pills to swallow a long time ago. I was told by many of my favorite judges like Judge Debbie O'Dell-Seneca that a good settlement is one that makes both sides unhappy. I also understood going into this case that my parents once advised me that not every one of my clients in a case like this would be happy.

I had made peace with the settlement in large part because it did help those most injured. However, I was not about to give in and let those who had good cases walk away and simply accept this deal. Some guys who were diagnosed with CTE through the PET scan rejected the terms of the settlement. Other guys simply appreciated the fact that CTE was not covered and were satisfied risking it all to wait until they die and have their brains tested and continue their fight in court. However, when it was all said and done to accept or reject, my clients had a resounding acceptance rate over 95 percent.

The uncapped settlement brought many new lawyers out of the woodwork. It resulted in them offering the players seriously reduced fee percentages and promises of even better results if they signed with them. With them, they also brought pre-settlement payments to the players which caused a great deal of controversy.

In November of 2014, Judge Brody allowed for a final approval hearing to review the terms of the settlement for adequacy, reasonableness, and fairness. There were a number of objectors who felt that the settlement was unfair. However, it was clear from the tone of the argument that Judge Brody planned to approve the settlement.

The expectation was that, barring any lengthy appeals, payment of the brain injured players would commence in 2015. But the reality is that a battle was only beginning.

CHAPTER 42

Smaller Target

In 2014, life as a lawyer took me down a path of new litigation. I recall receiving a phone call from Steve Fainaru, a Pulitzer Prize author who was working for ESPN at that time. Steve and his brother, Mark, wrote *League of Denial*, which uncovered many of the corrupt actions of the NFL involving brain-injured football players. Steve called and started with small talk, asking what I was working on given the NFL settlement. I told Steve that I was working on a lawsuit against the NCAA. Steve said, "Maybe you ought to go after smaller targets at some point."

Matt Onyshko e-mailed me out of the blue like many others have in the past. The message was brief and to the point. Matt said, "I am thirty-two years old, I played college football at California University of Pennsylvania, and I have ALS." I was immediately curious. I knew there were some of the same class-action lawyers from the NFL case involved with working on a class-action settlement that would offer a coupon to anyone who ever played an NCAA sport to get a free medical evaluation. But there was no lawyer litigating for neurologically damaged former NCAA players concerning the NCAA's responsibility as to brain injury on collegiate sports.

I was instantly intrigued by what I could uncover. I immediately read more medical journals. I was pointed to documents showing that university doctors were studying football brain injuries and helmet technology in the 1960s, yet they never shared the harmful results with any of the amateur athletes. In 1933, the NCAA produced a sports medical handbook that discussed the need to sit out concussed athletes for weeks. In that same medical publication, they discussed "punch drunk," which was related to repeated head trauma experienced by boxers and football players. There it was in black and white. The NCAA, despite its years of governing collegiate athletics and creating scientific and medical committees to protect the health and safety of amateur athletes, failed to disclose the dangers of head hits.

I soon thereafter filed Matt Onyshko's case against the NCAA and began the litigation and discovery process. As expected, the NCAA came out swinging. They immediately tried to have the entire case dismissed, arguing that they have no legal duty to protect the safety and health of collegiate athletes. Rather, they argued that responsibility fell on the colleges to protect the athletes. Judge Kathy Emery of Washington County, Pennsylvania, strongly disagreed and reasoned that the NCAA had an obligation to its athletes that extended to a legal duty to protect the safety of kids playing college sports.

Once we got past the initial hurdle, we started the discovery phase of the case. Again, we were confronted with more roadblocks. At this stage, I had help from my partner, Diana Jacobs, investigating the awareness of the NCAA's representatives on this topic. The NCAA first dumped on us thousands of documents. They were produced to us as one-page pictures. It was as if we had to piece together a ten-thousand-piece puzzle before we could even decipher what information was in the NCAA's corporate records. After having our team review these documents, it was obvious that many relevant pieces of the puzzle were not produced by the NCAA's army of lawyers.

One of my assistants, Amy Dorin, brought to our attention that the NCAA housed an online library and hard-copy library of records dating back many decades. So long as someone made an appointment with the librarian, they were welcome to review any copy any materials. After scheduling an appointment, I alerted the NCAA's lawyers of our intention to go to the library at the NCAA's headquarters in Indianapolis. This professional courtesy was met with a motion to sanction my law firm and me and requested disciplinary sanctions including termination of my license to practice law. This meant two things. First, this case was going to be contested every step of the way. Second, it solidified the fact that my litigation was the biggest threat to these football organizations. Otherwise, what was there to hide?

While continuing through discovery, it became clear that it would take a number of lawyers, staff, and a lot of money to properly put this massive case together against the NCAA. By way of example, the task of taking the deposition of one former NCAA Executive required combing through documents and information from the NCAA's archives dating back to 1909. Reviewing and pulling out the most pertinent information from the volumes of rulebooks, handbooks, and correspondence amongst the various departments and staff within the NCAA would be as difficult as asking an individual to read, retain, and understand all of the information contained in all of the volumes of an encyclopedia. It wasn't a task that I could handle by myself, let alone accomplish with one other lawyer, paralegal, and assistant. When I realized the help that I needed, I turned to our firm's managing partner, Bruce Mattock, to assist with the situation. Bruce Mattock decided, as a managing partner at my law firm, to bring in a young talented firm he was friendly with who had a ton of experience handling complex cases with many trials. Therefore, Justin Shrader's firm out of Houston, Texas, soon became our equal partners to bring Matt's case to trial. In addition to working with a larger firm from Texas, I also enlisted the assistance of another young, hungry lawyer from Pittsburgh with a decade of trial experience who had just started his own firm, Max Petrunya. I first met Max through our assistance with mock trial at our law school alma mater, Duquesne University. We then reconnected when Max and I were inducted into the same class of a prestigious trial lawyers' organization in the Pittsburgh area. At 31 years old, Max was the youngest lawyer in the organizations 50-year history to be inducted into the Academy of Trial Lawyers. Through our friendship I recognized that Max shared my passion for helping people and my work ethic. When the opportunity presented itself for me to invite Max to work with me on the NCAA litigation, he jumped at the opportunity. Max and

I have spent countless hours pouring through historical documents and information from the NCAA in the name of helping individuals like Matt Onyshko, and all other former college football players who have been harmed by the failures of the NCAA.

By the time Justin's firm started to roll up their sleeves, I already started filing more NCAA cases around the country. Thom Geishauser was a defensive back who played for legendary Coach Bobby Bowden. Coach Bowden testified that Thom sustained the hardest hit he ever saw in his coaching career, which left Thom with a shattered helmet and unconscious. Thom's case was filed in Morgantown, West Virginia, where Thom played for the Mountaineers in the late 60s and early 70s. A lawsuit on behalf of Kerry Goode, who is living with ALS, was filed in Atlanta, Georgia. Kerry was a co-captain and star running back for the University of Alabama. I also filed a lawsuit for Chuck Schretzman in Philadelphia. Chuck, a decorated lt. colonel and army veteran, played as a standout linebacker for the US Military Academy. Chuck, as well, suffers from ALS.

At that same time these cases were progressing, I received a call from Deb Ploetz. Deb's husband, Greg Ploetz, died from stage 4 CTE. He was a standout defensive lineman for the University of Texas. He was part of the 1969 national championship team. After school, Greg became an art teacher, husband, and loving father until his life slipped away from him starting in his late fifties. He ended up with dementia, confusion, anger, aggression, and required assisted living until his death. Our team filed this case in Dallas, Texas.

Judge Ken Molberg fast-tracked the case for trial. Ultimately, it was scheduled for trial in June 2018. During the discovery phase, Gene Egdorf from Justin Shrader's office was able to have the newly appointed medical director of the NCAA, Dr. Brian Hainline, acknowledge that CTE, ALS, and other neurodegenerative diseases were linked to repeated trauma from playing football. The key witness in the case was Dr. Bennet Omalu. I brought my friend, Bennet, into the case to allow him an opportunity to testify how football killed Greg Ploetz and for how long the NCAA and the NFL have denied, ignored, and concealed the fact that football caused later-life brain damage. In the fifth day of trial, Deb's case for her late husband concluded.

Ultimately, Matt Onyshko's case tried over the course of four weeks in Washington County, Pennsylvania. Shortly before trial, Judge Michael Lucas was assigned to replace Judge Emery, who was on medical leave. Dr. Bennet Omalu testified brilliantly as to the cause of Matt Onyshko's ALS being from football. The jurors loved him and, unified, stated that he was the best witness of over forty witnesses in the entire case. However, because of rulings by Judge Lucas that kept the experts from mentioning CTE during trial, the jury did not find in favor of Matt Onyshko. Those legal issues are now on appeal.

However, whether it be Ploetz, Goode, Shretzman, or Matt Onyshko, the NCAA will continue to face former college athletes one by one in a courtroom to determine their culpability for hiding the dangers of repetitive trauma from football players for decades.

CHAPTER 43

False Start

Meanwhile, Chris Seeger had promised that the NFL settlement would provide instant relief to the players and families who need it most. That was never to happen. Rather, the proposed settlement ended up tied up for nearly thirty months while appeals were fought all the way up to the United States Supreme Court.

Lawyers were coming in late to the case in an effort to better the settlement. Their hope was to get the true disease CTE paid under the deal. The NFL lawyers and Chris Seeger quickly responded that all the symptoms of CTE would be covered in the dementia diagnoses that paid the former players. All the courts agreed and shot down the effort to get players paid for a CTE diagnosis whether living or dead, despite CTE—the disease of repeated head trauma—being the heart of the case and the disease of the former NFL players.

While the appeals were unfolding, the full-frontal attacks continued by late-coming lawyers and their agents. These lawyers were promising to obtain a diagnosis which would pay the players substantially under the settlement agreement if they fired their original lawyers and signed their half-priced contracts hiring them. But the catch didn't stop there. Some lawyers promised pre-settlement advances on their claims while others handed players an envelope of cash walking into appointments, with hand-picked doctors scheduled to examine them at their lawyer's office. The most despicable of all was one lawyer who actually swindled pension money and savings accounts from his clients. This lawyer is now fighting to save himself from jail for his treatment of former NFL players.

Out of nowhere, I started receiving termination letters from some of my clients. They all appeared professionally written and asked for their complete files and expenses to date. I had no choice but to comply. However, I warned each of the now-former clients that greener pastures did not await them. Rather, I predicted that this scheme would be sniffed out at the end of the day, and they would be left without adequate representation. I was correct, but it took a ton of effort and considerable time before these unscrupulous actions were addressed.

Having never been involved in mass tort multidistrict litigation before, I was entirely unaware of companies offering pre-settlement advances of injury victims such as hernia mesh cases or 911 victim lawsuits. The lending companies attacked in flocks like vultures on a dead animal. They fast-talked the cognitively impaired former NFL players who were hard up for money. The lenders offered tens of thousands of dollars in loans within twenty-four hours of signing their agreements, which had rates starting at 25 percent and as high as 100 percent per year. Some of these lending companies affiliated with law firms with plans to take the entire anticipated settlement award from the player in exchange for loaning a much smaller amount immediately.

Stunned by all of these happenings, I reached out directly to Chris Seeger to express my concerns. I wanted to let him know that I believed the conduct of the lawyers was unethical, the loans were usurious and, as lead counsel, how was he going to curtail these efforts? I was shocked when he told me that these lenders show up in every mass tort, and historically, they just signed off, acknowledging their loans as liens to the file which would be paid off when the claim was awarded. I was left with the option of losing clients one by one in the hundreds or complying with the wishes of those who needed loans immediately.

Ultimately, many of my clients entered into these high-interest settlement advances against my law firm's advice. Eventually, this issue caught the attention of Judge Brody when one of the lending companies was taken to court in New York by the attorney general for allegedly predatory loans offered to 911 victims as well as former NFL players.

Judge Brody was called upon to determine whether all the loans of the players were in violation of the settlement agreement. Specifically, the settlement agreement stated that no player could assign his claim to another party. Judge Brody ruled that the lending contracts contained language which appeared to assign their claims to the lending companies. Therefore, she ruled every contract to be a prohibited assignment and invalid. It left me scratching my head how Chris Seeger could have told me to just sign off on those deals. Years later, a lending company challenged this ruling on appeal. The Third Circuit Court of Appeals found that Judge Brody did not have the authority to invalidate those contracts.

In the meantime, we received a notification from Chris Seeger's office to turn in our time records for purposes of dividing up the common benefit money set aside to compensate the lawyers for their efforts on behalf of all former players. Prior to Seeger being lead counsel, I had spent half a decade and thousands of hours pulling together this lawsuit that he settled over a matter of a few months. I prepared those hours in a declaration that was also substantiated by personal declarations from Dr. Bennet Omalu, Mike Webster's disability lawyer Bob Fitzsimmons, and others who were intimately aware of my work. Holding true to form, Chris Seeger rejected the entire submission as not providing a benefit to the players. To pour salt into the wound, he also cut nearly half of my hours for work that I performed after 2012.

Chris Seeger ultimately put together a petition to disburse the common benefit money of $112,000,000 that directed nearly $70,000,000 to him alone. Because of many objections by lawyers, Judge Brody assigned a law professor from Harvard to advise her on how to disburse the Common Benefit Fund fairly to the lawyers. When it was all said and done, $90,000,000 of the fund was awarded. My law firm was awarded only $325,000. Judge Brody did note that our award was increased to that amount due to our early efforts and my relationship with Bennet Omalu. Nonetheless, Chris

Seeger's law firm was awarded $51,000,000 and they continue to bill approximately $1,000,000 worth of legal work per quarter which will quickly deplete the remaining $20,000,000 solely for his law firm's benefit.

While the battle over lawyer fees was taking place, Judge Brody ordered that we turn over all pending contracts with our clients and any communications with lending companies. This literally required me to look through every client file in hard copy and electronic as well as e-mails sent to lawyers and staff from clients or lending companies. Due to the massive nature and ethical concerns involving communications with clients, I contracted in experienced lawyers Michael DeMarco and Kiersten Lane to advise and assist with this monstrous undertaking. When it was all said and done, we had nearly two boxes of papers to file and a lot of time and expense which nearly wiped away the $325,000 award to my law firm.

Meanwhile, Judge Brody ruled that some of the player lending contracts were invalid while others were, in fact, standard loan agreements. It is hard to overstate the lack of sophistication of the players in dealing with a multi-million dollar loan company. Therefore, with the assistance of the claims administrators, the special masters, she appointed the Locks firm to sort through these contracts in the best interests of the players. Gene Locks and David Langfitt turned out to be solid advocates for the players in this platform as well as upholding the fairness of the agreement to the benefit of the players.

On the flip side, my predictions on bad lawyering proved to be completely accurate. Judge Brody found that lending companies were, in fact, teaming together with law firms and fabricating diagnoses and offering small loans for selling over their entire settlement. Ultimately, Judge Brody ordered a special prosecutor appointed to explore all viable options including even criminal convictions. This terrible lawyering by a small group of bad apples left a lasting stain on the good lawyers who had the player's and their family's best interests at heart.

During this period of time, while the appeals were being decided, it solidified my beliefs of our civil justice system. First, if you want to expect justice, it can only be obtained for fighting on behalf of one injured person at a time. Second, class actions provide no real justice for injured parties, just the lawyers. Third, if I ever was to get involved in a class action in the future, I would only do it as lead counsel.

CHAPTER 44

The Benefit to the Retired Players

Finally, as of January 2017, the NFL settlement was declared final, approved, and binding after all appeals were exhausted. However, it still took months before claims could be filed for payment or players could go to one of the approved doctors for testing.

Even after months passed and former players were able to submit claims for their diagnoses, it became even clearer that the settlement was designed to make it nearly impossible for players or families to qualify for payments. For starters, the claim form was over ten pages in length, and the form required to be completed and signed by the diagnosing physician was seventeen pages in length.

The next hurdle came shortly thereafter during the review process when the claims administrator declared over half of the claims deficient as they wanted more medical records. The reality was that the NFL did not expect over 1,500 claims filed by the entire class of retired players within months. Therefore, the NFL immediately requested that the terms of the settlement be re-reviewed, clarified, or amended. As a result, most claims were held pending resolution of those issues which took upwards of six more months. The solution required the implementation of a frequently asked question summary to be produced. The summary itself was hundreds of questions and answers in length.

Ultimately, I did start to receive award notices for my clients, but only for about one-third of those filed claims. Many of the guys had to test again. Some of the awards received had to be fought through meritless NFL appeals simply to delay payment to the players and families. After all, their ability to do so was without limit, and if they could pay less claims, that meant more money stays with the league.

Then audits for many of the claims started. These audits came about because of the fraudulent claims pieced together by some of these shady late-coming lawyers backed by lending company money. Their actions spilled over to every single law firm who had to defend their standard expert work up of each case. It even happened with one of my experts, who simply made a diagnosis in thirty-four clients of mine out of the hundred that he had evaluated. However, the audit was closed with no misrepresentation or wrongdoing on any single client of mine.

The NFL mounted a limitless audit process to challenge these brain-injured players. One example happened to an individual who was driving and followed by a private investigator. When the player became concerned for his safety, he called the police. The police pulled over the investigator, who lied and said he was seeking an autograph despite having pictures and videos tracking the former player around for hours. Another example of a frivolous audit occurred to a former player who was determined to have dementia by four separate doctors. The NFL still did not want to pay the guy, so they searched his Facebook posts. They found one post that said he was selected to be on celebrity chef, but they failed to read the commentary that the post was a joke in support of autism awareness.

If the process wasn't enough to cause frustration and a drain of resources, the collection of funds was even worse. Players and families were asking why it was taking so long to send them payments. On top of that, they weren't happy that a large chunk of their award was being paid to health insurance companies for past services provided. Additionally, Judge Brody decided to place a hold on the lawyer's fees pending completion of a number of audits as well as her determination of fees permissible as contingent awards.

After many months of battling, it was determined that the lawyers who represented individual clients could receive up to 22 percent of the value of the client's award. But there was a catch. Five percent of that amount would be held to determine whether there were sufficient funds for class counsel to oversee the settlement. In total, after all of these efforts, I stood to collect maybe 22 percent of any claims which I received awards, but more likely, my firm would collect 17 percent of awards to our clients and share those fees with Tom Girardi and Herman Russomanno.

Thankfully, I was able to achieve awards for over seventy clients and it continues to grow. Over the next decade, it seems reasonable that those figures could reach over one hundred players. This will require monitoring the players and continuing to schedule neurological and neuropsychological examinations for years to come. In the meantime, they all require assistance from our Medicare system to care for their health needs, as the NFL settlement has only compensated roughly 700 former players from the group of 20,000 who played in the NFL.

Nonetheless, the claims process is filled with obstacles and loopholes throughout the entire process. For instance, the audit process uncovered outrageous conduct in the medical report process. One group of lawyers used a doctor who evaluated hundreds of patients and paid the doctors for over thirty-five hours of work on one workday. Another group of lawyers paid the doctors on a results-only contingency. In other words, the more and greater the possible award payment, the greater the doctor would be paid. Lastly, there were other lawyers setting up doctors to evaluate dozens of clients daily at a hotel room. All of these actions tainted the legitimate claims and forced Judge Brody to appoint a special investigator to prosecute those corrupt actions.

Another prime example to show the players are not being taken care of in this settlement is a client of mine who was awarded worker's compensation benefits from a team and insurance carrier after battling in court over three decades ago. This resulted in hundreds of thousands of dollars of medical care having to be paid for by the insurance carrier who lost. When he received an award in the NFL case, this insurance company, who not only insured the team but also the league, asked for over a half-million dollars paid back to them. Despite asking the NFL and Seeger to step in, which they failed to do, I was able to protect my client in the end.

One thing that remains open for this case is the status of the claims of Mike Webster, Terry Long, and Justin Strzelczyk. They were the three former Pittsburgh Steelers who were diagnosed with CTE by Dr. Omalu. Unfortunately, their claims were left outside looking in during the negotiation process. Because they died prior to January 2006, the settlement required that these families jump through an extra hoop to show that their legal claims should be paid despite the players' long-ago deaths. Despite the claims process opening in April of 2017, these families are still waiting for the decision on their claims.

CHAPTER 45

Future of Collision Sports

One unintentional but anticipated result occurred as a result of my NFL lawsuit. Less kids are signing up to play football. Pop Warner football league's recent reports showed that 10 percent to 30 percent less kids are playing tackle football. Parents are refusing to get their kids involved in football due to fear that they may have later life brain damage. The first goal of the lawsuit was not to end football but to educate future generations to play the game safely so they don't have chronic brain damage.

Former President Obama was quoted as saying, "I would not let my son play pro football." However, he remarked that today's players, "they know what they're buying into. It is no longer a secret. It's sort of the feeling I have about smokers, you know?"

The reality remains that sub-concussions and concussions are a major public health threat of the twenty-first century. The key issue for me is that the children need to be properly taken care of as they are in no position to make an informed decision involving later life brain injury while they are minors.

At birth, the brain weighs a mere 350 grams. At the age of two, the brain is about 75 percent of its adult size. The brain reaches almost 95 percent of its adult size by the age of ten. It does not ultimately reach its adult size until the age of eighteen to twenty-four in humans. Therefore, until then, the brain is a developing brain.

Not surprisingly, an injury to the brain prior to age twenty-four can result in more serious and permanent injury. This means that the brains of children who play contact sports such as football are more vulnerable to the sub-concussions and concussive impacts that are directly connected with the sport. This could result in a child who plays those sports being prevented from attaining full cognitive, intellectual, and functional abilities as an adult.

Many folks are unaware that there have been studies conducted of prisoners which have been published in many prominent medical journals that show that over 60 percent of the prison populations studied show a history of traumatic brain injury. One study I was personally involved with the Brain Injury Association of Pennsylvania showed a Pennsylvania prison that revealed over 70 percent of prisoners had a history of traumatic brain injury.

Football continues to set new ratings records with no end in sight for the popularity of the NFL. Sponsors pay exorbitant sums of money to attach themselves to the league broadcasts. There are billions of dollars in television contract deals with the league and the major broadcasting networks. It does not appear that watching the NFL or NCAA will slow.

The sport has become a mecca of entertainment. The game now includes pyrotechnics, much like the world of professional wrestling. Merchandising has exploded the brand of teams and game breaker players. More and more money is being spent on fantasy football and gambling, which is now permitted in every state. The league may someday reach its goal of having international teams and have over $25 billion in profits per year.

However, anyone that believes that football's future is secure needs to think back to the popularity of boxing. In the early 1900s through the 1980s, boxing was the world's most popular sport, drawing huge crowds and international attention. Boxing events on pay-per-view would charge $50 per customer to watch the championship bouts.

Muhammad Ali and many other boxers began suffering from later-life brain damage. This made the problems too hard to ignore. There were also reports of abuse, fights, and drugs in certain fighters, most notably the domestic violence related to Mike Tyson. Regardless of the sport's popularity, many people stopped watching regardless of their passion for the sport.

I don't believe that the NFL is destined to the same path of boxing. However, the sport remains in a vulnerable state. Many others thought that smoking would never become taboo. Others, like those in my legal profession, never thought that asbestos would be taken out of the steel industry. Asbestos was the best and cheapest form of insulation for the extreme temperatures. However, boxing, smoking, and asbestos have largely disappeared from our country. Football isn't doomed to that path, but the sport is not invulnerable either. Just imagine if you told your parents and grandparents that someday their grandchildren would not be able to name boxing's heavyweight champion of the world.

If you ask my 500-plus clients, they would tell you, one for all and all for one, that they would have done it all again and played in the NFL. They just simply wanted a chance to take care of their brains. If the trainers, physicians, and league would simply put in reasonable protocol to have the players removed from games and practices after sustaining a concussion until their brains repair, then those actions would be satisfactory. Certainly, there are rule changes that have improved the sport from helmet-to-helmet contact. However, any rule that prohibits the sudden acceleration and deceleration forces will save today's players from those later-life problems.

I was recently a part of a panel discussing the concussion lawsuit. The one thing that grabbed my attention was that a lawyer congratulated me on changing litigation for all times. He described the NFL case as a landmark case. Concussion injuries and brain injuries were arriving in every personal injury lawsuit as a new injury from simple slip and falls to devastating auto accident cases. What used to be called a whiplash is now being correctly classified as a concussion that requires ongoing appropriate care and treatment.

My fear of the NFL lawsuit was that bad lawyers would attempt to apply the same legal theories to other sports which did not apply and did not have the same factual basis for such claims. That fear happened. A few years after the NFL litigation, a group of lawyers filed suit against the National Hockey League, arguing that they failed to implement proper protocols to handle the concussed NHL player. I am guessing they never heard my radio show praising the NHL for actually putting in place concussion guidelines requiring independent physician release some twenty years earlier. Maybe they were unfamiliar with Sidney Crosby, the world's greatest player of this generation, who sat out nearly 320 days due to his battle with a concussion. They ultimately settled the case for payout of $22,000 for each player, even those that died from CTE.

Other lawyers have filed suit against the World Wresting Entertainment Company, seeking damages for a class of former wrestlers who suffered brain damage. Even some lawyers in Canada got involved by suing the Canadian Football League for cognitive problems of the professional football players in Canada. I heard of cases of rugby players in other countries for this brain injury problems. Recently it has been brought to my attention that lawyers are attempting to file claims for actors in football movies who have allegedly suffered brain injury. While it is nice to recognize that my efforts in the NFL litigation have brought awareness to the public at large regarding the dangers of repetitive trauma to the brain, my hope is that these bad lawsuits brought by poor and inexperienced lawyers seeking to make a quick buck will not cause the media and the public to misconstrue and misinterpret the intent of the NFL litigation and question the scientific findings regarding repetitive trauma and neurodegenerative disease.

My firm and those in the asbestos world have always wondered what would be the next biggest trend in litigation. The question that always arose concerned whether any type of negligence would ever hit the mass population like asbestos did. We are certainly at its early stages, but it appears that brain injury in sports is certainly a growing area of civil litigation.

Recently, some lawyers in Illinois have taken the fight to high school football organizations. They are seeking to tackle the associations that feed the NFL for their improper handling of concussions in the youth. This is a serious threat to the future of the game.

Concussion problems have not just stayed in America. The publicity from this case has taken off in Canada, Mexico, and Spain and as far as Australia. There have been articles expressing potential threats of litigation in these countries' sports related to concussion problems.

Football is not the only sport that faces concussion concerns as I discussed. However, it is a growing health crisis that requires attention in all sports from lacrosse to soccer to field hockey to water polo. Believe it or not, water polo had the most reported concussions in Pennsylvania's sports recently.

Less than a handful of years ago, no one knew that a concussion was a concern. Today, the public has been put on notice of concussion injuries and face decisions identical to those that were made with smoking. However, the decision was simpler and easier with smoking as smoking tastes bad. Sports, on the other hand, taste like mom's apple pie.

It is essential that we apply the best rules to promote safety to protect the brain. Even with the best rules, it is inevitable that concussions will occur. Therefore, it is imperative that we focus on proper playing techniques. On top of that, the focus needs to include equipment that is more absorbent of impacts. I recently came across a skull cap and headband make by 2nd Skull that reduced impacts by 35 percent on average.

We also need to have better medical diagnostic devices that can diagnose a brain injury more objectively. I recently learned of such a device that can measure brain cognitively and functioning ability from the age of five until death. This device is a twelve-minute web-based test that scores you throughout your lifetime, and an even shorter version called the Roberto app can be used on your smart phone. It was developed in Pittsburgh and sponsored by the family of the greatest sports humanitarian of all time, Roberto Clemente. The RC21X device will change the platform of brain health monitoring in the next decade.

Above and beyond this, we must continue our focus on developing prophylactic and curative interventions, including pharmacologic interventions for concussion related injuries. The goal being to find a cure for chronic traumatic encephalopathy. But to do that, we must let the scientists continue to autopsy the brains of those who played any type of contact sport and not hide critical scientific data.

CHAPTER 46

The Future

Since I started exploring this case at the age of thirty, there has been an avalanche of change that has occurred all around me.

I do not talk about the NFL case with my friends unless they ask. They all have this belief that I just walked into hundreds of millions of dollars. This could not be further from the truth. Today, I make sure I spend more time with my hobbies than I did in the first dozen years of my legal career. I spend more time trying to hone my golf skills. I also enjoy spending time in the gym and riding my bikes. I have completed seven 100k bike rides and competitive runs as well.

As a lawyer, the one thing that gives me great pride is hearing congratulations on my origination of the case by other lawyers. I have heard from some of the heads of the major lawyer organizations. I heard from the American Bar Association. I heard from the chair of the Public Justice Foundation, thanking me for my efforts to make the profession honorable. It made me realize that there are still many lawyers who make the profession an honorable profession of integrity. My personal favorite message was hearing from Joe Rice. Joe was the late Ron Motley's partner. Ron was the guy who took down the tobacco industry and was featured by Russell Crowe in *The Insider* movie. Joe offered the highest praise when he said that Ron would be proud of me for successfully taking on a matter of civil justice. I am sure that he wishes that he would have been aware that his law firm could have been hand-in-hand with me in this case from the beginning.

Tom Girardi, Herman Russomanno, and Bob Borrello have leaned heavily on my efforts to make the most of our NFL clients claims while we wait to continue our case against Riddell.

My clients have become some of my best friends. In this world of texting, many of them always keep in touch. Some have legal problems and questions. Others simply want to send me prayers and well wishes. I consider many of them friends that will outlive this case. There are so many I haven't mentioned, but some of the most uplifting thoughts and prayers have come from Vernon Maxwell, the late Rick Jones, Maurice Spencer, George Visger, Lou Lipps, Mark Gastineau, Leonard Marshall, Bernard Ford, and Tony Dorsett. They remain appreciative for the fight that was brought on their behalf.

Dr. Omalu and I remain friends to this day. He introduces me to others as the only person that believed in him. I introduce him as the most famous doctor in the world that changed the world and saved the lives of many former football players along with way.

The NFL still employs Elliot Pellman as an advisor. Since the concussion case has been filed, he has not spoken a single word. Former NFL Commissioner Paul Taglibue was recently selected to the NFL Hall of Fame despite being in charge of the league while the NFL's Mild Traumatic Brain Injury Committee was manufacturing false science and data on repetitive trauma and brain injuries. It is perplexing that a former commissioner that supervised this conduct which players relied on when making the decision to risk life and limb for the sport can be chosen for football's highest honor. On the other hand, Dr. Joe Maroon continues to be the leading neurologist of the Pittsburgh Steelers. He personally reached out to Dr. Omalu to express his being wrong on this issue. Despite hundreds of published papers confirming the link between trauma and chronic brain damage, the NFL and NCAA's agents continue to dispute the unanimous science on the subject. NFL and NCAA need taken to task by those powers in our country employed with such authority.

For my clients who died to put a name to the problem of former football players, Mike Webster, Terry Long, and Justin Strzelczyk, their families still await their day in court to hopefully receive a monetary award for all of their sacrifices.

Chuck Schretzman, Kerry Goode, and many other former collegiate players and families will soon have their day in court, one by one, against the NCAA's failures to protect their amateur athletes.

On a personal note, the death of my mom really shook up our family structure. When we are together, there is a definite emptiness. My brother and I have done a good job of taking my father on different trips to keep him company. He, as well, has helped himself by finding a new companion and remarrying. My grandmother, Mom's mom, passed away peacefully at the age of eighty-nine. My grandmother, Dad's mom, died from Alzheimer's disease in her mid-nineties. My brother and I remain close to this very day.

My wife and I decided to move our family to Hilton Head Island in South Carolina in June of 2016. It was necessary to get out of the Pittsburgh area and start a new beginning. After all, my clients and cases are all over the country. Hilton head became our new small town, which ironically has also been home to John Mellencamp. My daughters, Addison and Alexis, are now twelve and eleven. They are mainly straight-A students at their prep school across the street from our modest home. Addison enjoys ballet and dance and has performed in a number of shows already even as a co-lead. Alexis golfs and cheers. My girls are always studying, going to activities, or practicing their instruments every day. My wife has remained my best supporter. She continues to be my go-to person for my legal and practical advice on work matters. However, football or my football cases are not a topic we are allowed to discuss.

For me, this case has led me to many new medical malpractice and personal injury cases of families seeking a lawyer to support a cause. I work on those cases with the same passion I put into every past case. The cases now seem bigger and even sadder. I hope injured parties do their homework and not just hire someone on television but, instead, hire those with passion, interest, and results when seeking compensation for their serious injuries and deaths.

My passion with brain injury has helped me perform pro-bono work for the Pennsylvania Brain Injury Association as well as travelling the country lecturing and teaching on brain-injured clients. I have done lecturers for both of my alma maters already. I hope this story becomes the required reading of anyone who aspires to go to law school or is already in law school.

Education surrounding awareness and prevention and safety matters needs more public attention. We need to provide those without the means of professional athletes that are playing the same contact sports the opportunity for the same safety measures, doctoring, and education as the professional leagues. We must educate all associations, schools, leagues, coaches, trainers, and even universities on these great games that are played in our country but to do so in a very safe manner. It's our obligation as a society to protect each other. I see it as our duty to continue as Moses on the matter of concussion in sports.

Speaking of Moses, after all of those years of battling, I received a call recently from Vernon Maxwell. I picked up the phone and said my greetings. The first words out of his mouth were "Omalu was right." He said, "You know what I am talking about, don't you? Omalu said, 'Let Jason be your Moses.' I want to thank you for what you did personally for me and so many other guys and their families. You are our Moses."

ACKNOWLEDGMENTS

This story would never be told without the efforts of Dr. Bennet Omalu to first discover CTE in the brains of former professional football players. We thank you for your vision to look deeper, and I thank you for entrusting me to vindicate your name through litigation and provide necessary help to many former players and families.

To the families of Mike Webster, Terry Long, Justin Strzelczyk, and Andre Waters, and every other client and former football player living and dead. May your hearts be blessed knowing that you suffered for a greater cause and that you be glorified in the truth.

To the members of the legal, medical, and scientific community who helped make this story. I appreciate your patience in sharing your knowledge, skill, and training with me so that I could use it to obtain justice. I remain grateful to you all.

To my coworkers and helpers, especially Cindy DeUnger, and my law firm who helped me seek justice despite all the obstacles. Thank you for guiding me and keeping me out of trouble.

To my co-counsel colleagues and friends I met along the journey. May you continue to do great things, and may God bless you abundantly.

To my friends and family. Without you, there would be no book. You are an inspiration to me to never give up even when told that I should give up. Just don't give up!

A special thank you to everyone at Christian Faith Publishing for their help and support to complete this book. I am also grateful to Max Petrunya, Shelly Pagac, Michael DeMarco, Cindy DeUnger and Kelly Luckasevic for their assistance, advice and guidance in finishing my story.

To my wife and daughters. I am blessed every day that you are in my life. You provide purpose and motivation to push me to be better. I thank you for being with me through good and bad in every step of this journey.

To everyone else, especially everyone I should have mentioned in this book and those who read it, I want you to know that I believe we are all one family of mankind. With our love and Christ's blessings, we can care for one another to make this a safer and loving home. I wish you every happiness, peace, and joy.

ABOUT THE AUTHOR

Jason Luckasevic is a trial lawyer headquartered in Pittsburgh. He started the lawsuit against the NFL for their failure to properly handle brain damage in their former players and continues to litigate against other sports organizations. He also maintains a full-time litigation practice helping individuals with serious injuries caused by other individuals or corporations. He now lives on Hilton Head Island with his wife Kelly and their two daughters Addison and Alexis.